For Sue —
Make your
Miracles
~~HAPA~~

HOW TO MAKE A MIRACLE

Also by M. Gary Neuman

Helping Your Kids Cope With Divorce the Sandcastles Way (Random House)

Emotional Infidelity, How to Affair-Proof Your Marriage and Other Secrets to a Great Relationship (Crown)

How To Make a Miracle

Finding Incredible Spirituality in Times of Happiness and Struggle

Rabbi M. Gary Neuman

Pedmy Press

Copyright © 2006 by G.K.N. Corporation

All rights reserved. No part of this book may be reproduced or transmitted in any form or by any means, electronic or mechanical, including photocopying, recording, or by any information storage and retrieval system, without permission in writing from the author.

Published by ⌊Pedmy Press

Printed in the United States of America
ISBN 1-59872-367-7

First Paperback Edition

To my Soulmate,
Michal Leah

Contents

Introduction	1
Part One:	
Understanding Who You Really Are	5
Can We Prove This Soul Exists	13
Follow the Dreams Worth Dreaming	44
Finding Your Soul	48
Developing Your Eternal Self	85
Rebecca, Navigating Life Through Kindness	129
Part Two:	
Setting Up Your Day for Spirituality	142
Morning, the Beginning of Everything-Kindness	145
Afternoon, Blending Spiritual and Corporeal Self-Real Strength	156
Nighttime, Seeing the Fire in the Dark	172

Part Three:
How You Will Change the World
and Everyone In It   181

Love Thy Neighbor As Thyself   199

Loving Yourself   218

Prayer   225

Death is Just Another Beginning   256

Epilogue   263

Introduction

Nothing is impossible.
Impossible might just take a little longer.

Spirituality is quite a challenge. Writing a book about it seems impossible. It almost assumes there is some finite area of it that can conform to the written page. And so my personal challenge to share my version, my journey, if you will, of my sense of spirituality began. How do I show you what I see? How do I share that delightful moment when I'm breathing through my soul, when everything makes sense? How do I help you find your own unique version of the same? With this seemingly insurmountable challenge I began writing and found that it was easier than I thought. As spirituality has a habit of doing, once I allowed myself to focus on it, it flowed rather easily and I've had the pleasure of growing through the experience.

There was another concern in writing this book. Here's the deal. In today's world, spirituality is divided into two camps. Religion-God based while the other is person centered-finding a soul within. Unfortunately, I can't separate the two which can cause great alarm to many. Just the word "God" can throw readers into a frightened tizzy. I do use this term and I do discuss characters from the Bible (I use "Torah" throughout to refer to the five books of Moses). But my intention is only to get you to the place I've been, a place deep within you that requires you to build your own personal connectedness to spirituality and the world around you. I may talk about God but as you'll see, "God" is what you will make of it. It is a name that you will largely define and that definition will likely be quite different than mine and others. With this in mind, I've written this book for those both far and near from religion and spirituality.

Yes, I am a rabbi and yes I use the Torah as a source for my spiritual search. But don't confuse me for someone who has a specific religious agenda. Allow yourself to hear some of the meaningful lessons I've gleaned from ancient stories having little to do with whether you believe them as true or not. I'm not asking you to believe *them*. But I am asking you to believe in *you*. You are a miracle and within you is the key to creating many more miracles than you realize.

E=MC2=YOU

There are many explanations to Einstein's Theory of Relativity. But for me it comes down to this description by Bill Bryson in his book, *A Short History of Nearly Everything.*

"In simplest terms, what the equation says is that mass and energy have an equivalence. They are two forms of the same thing: energy is liberated matter; matter is energy waiting to happen. Since C2 (the speed of light times itself) is a truly enormous number, what the equation is saying is that there is a huge amount, a really huge amount of energy bound up in every material thing. You may not feel outstandingly robust, but if you are an average-sized adult you will contain within your modest frame no less that 7 times 10 to the 18th power joules of potential energy-enough to explode with the force of thirty very large hydrogen bombs, assuming you knew how to liberate it and really wished to make a point."

Science has proven that you and I have unfathomable energy locked up inside us. This energy is waiting to be unleashed and your ability to unlock it speaks to your inner godliness. There are people who made a difference to this world more powerful than the impact of thirty large hydrogen bombs and others leave barely a trace of themselves. How much of your energy will impact the world?

Part One: Understanding Who You Really Are

Openness to Change.

Judaism follows the lunar calendar. This is hard for many to comprehend but yes, there is an entirely different calendar with its own set of months and dates. For example, Hanukah seems to appear at different times during the month of December. True, but it occurs on the same date of every year, the 25th of the Hebrew lunar month called Kislev. This is why all Jewish holidays begin at sundown, not really sundown as much as moonrise, I'd say. The problem is that the lunar calendar is a mess to upkeep. Believe it or not, every few years or so, there must be a leap year which consists of adding an entire month to adjust the lunar calendar. It loses almost thirty days every few years. It seems severely inconsistent, no match for the accuracy of the solar calendar and yet the Torah clearly points to the moon as the governing body of the spiritual calendar.

Our moon serves as the most primal teaching of life. When you stare at the moon tonight one thing is for sure: you will not be viewing the same thing you saw last night or what you'll see tomorrow. Our vision of the moon changes every night. This serves as our beacon of light. Gaze at the moon every night and wonder how you've changed from last night to this moment and how you will change before tomorrow's vision of the moon. Furthermore, it is no coincidence that the moon only reflects the light of the sun. Its change is dependant on another source. You and I as well reflect our godliness within. Left to ourselves without focusing on our fire of spirituality within, we are dark and cold. It is only as we connect to the immortal life within and around us that we can serve to reflect a light that can shine, like the moon, lighting up the sky in its darkest hour more boldly than the stars that carry far greater light but are too distant, too disconnected to share powerful light. *We change and the source of that change is drinking in outside sources that nourish our spiritual reflection.* We never stay the same. We're moving up or we're moving down. We are in constant motion proven by our atomic structure and our constant, involuntary brain, heart and organ activity. If we're not changing, we might as well be physically dead because this stage of life cannot offer us much without our complete desire to seek change. *Life is for the living. Live and be that beacon of enormous light, radiating insightful warmth in a world of darkness.*

How's Your Vision?

He was a boy of fourteen searching for wisdom. He loved to learn and became the most well known spiritual leader of the Jewish people in the twentieth century. In his own curious way, he wondered what his teacher did in the aged study hall after all the boys in the Yeshiva, rabbinic school, had left for the night. He must find out, he decided. He hid one night in a cabinet awaiting the arrival of this teacher, entering the empty room full of worn holy books and the scent of passionate voices still echoing off of the cold stone floor.

This was how Rabbi Wasserman in 1935 began to tell the story of his teacher, Rabbi Israel Kagan. Although Rabbi Wasserman was a genius in his own right, never did a meeting pass when he wasn't asked to share a story about his famed spiritual teacher. This day he visited a classroom of teens whose eyes grew wider as they heard about the famous rabbi.

"Rabbi Kagan's teacher came in quietly assuming no one was there. The young Israel barely breathed as he peeked through a tiny slit he made by opening the cabinet door ever so slightly. There his teacher stood over a lectern and opened a large volume of holy writings. He began to sway and sing aloud the ancient texts in a creative, spontaneous tune. Suddenly from nowhere a small flame sprang up around him. The teacher paid no attention and continued to learn and read while the mystical fire

Understanding Who You Really Are 9

slowly grew as it seemingly danced to the rhythms of the wise man's holy voice well into the early morning eventually engulfing him. Continuing for hours as the teacher melodically read the ancient words, the young boy watched only flames. Moments before the young men were to arrive for morning prayers the teacher closed the holy books instantly extinguishing the fire around him. And so, young Israel had learned of his teacher's greatness."

As amazing as this story was, the teens who listened intently were confused. One brave student asked the great Rabbi Wasserman the simple question others were thinking.

"Excuse me, and of course with only the greatest respect, but we asked for a story about your teacher Rabbi Kagan. This was a wonderful story about Rabbi Kagan's teacher, not Rabbi Kagan himself. Did I misunderstand the story?" he asked while the other teens slightly nodded in agreement.

"You did my friend. My story was not about Rabbi Kagan's teacher who learned nightly amidst a mystical flame. My story was about Rabbi Kagan, who at the tender age of 14 was able to *see* the flame."

How do they do it? Those who are so spiritual, you can just sense it about them, their aura, their warmth. Why was this young man able to see the flame when everyone else couldn't? And how much more is there that we could see but are blind to?

I always marvel at the mundane experience of sitting quietly when suddenly as the sun peeks through a window pane just right, a stream of light illuminates thousands of dust particles floating in front of me. Imagine those dust particles, real physical properties were right in front of my nose and yet I didn't see them-completely blind to them. I can't help but wonder what else is right in front of me that I don't see? This dust is my simplest metaphor for a world full of hidden treasures. There's a world we don't see and never will unless

Understanding Who You Really Are 11

we choose to work on ourselves from within. History keeps teaching us this lesson. There was a time when doctors didn't see the germs on their hands nor could anyone imagine that the entire world was made up of molecules in constant motion. What will be the next eye opening discovery and who will see it first? Maybe it'll be you. After all, there is no one like you. Exactly who are you? That is for you to decide. But know this. *All of us are living beings in constant motion. Spiritual vision is about what we choose to see and how we nurture those skills that will help us see what we haven't seen before and what many never will. We can have greater spiritual vision but we have to be looking for it and building on every moment.*

We do some of it already-see completely different things-but we often don't recognize that we can use our perspective as our strongest tool to develop ourselves. Imagine four people walking down the same street together. The artist marvels at how the angles of the taut telephone wires interrupt the vast horizon melding human ingenuity with nature. The child smiles as the daydream of swinging from the looping loose pieces of those telephone wires like the trapeze man overwhelms his senses. The older man breathes deeply as he closes his eyes and hears the pleasant melodies of the birds that are resting on the telephone wires reminding him of his pet bird as a youth. The lawyer sees a telephone wire sadly dangling with the potential to hurt someone-a law suit waiting to happen. All of them see the same wires, but they might as well be on different continents-their experiences are so completely dissimilar.

And so every moment of every day each of us envision different things. Every part of our senses is focusing on bits and pieces of life having to do with our personal life history. *Everything we've ever done or experienced works together to bring us to this very moment, every moment; to see, hear, touch, smell, taste...to feel life. It is in your soul that life is generated and continued forever. That soul is your key to living forever-And it is there that life can never be taken from you.* Every moment that you spend on your journey to your soul is a moment spent on eternity.

Can We Prove This Soul Exists?
Show Me the Miracle

Let's face it. It can be quite challenging to believe that there is anything godly in our world. So much tragedy. Everyone must wonder at some point how there can be such pain if in all of us is this spiritual source of peace and loving-kindness. We may use this seeming contradiction to restrain ourselves from so many wonderful spiritual moments. We can literally hold ourselves back from tapping into our deeper spiritual selves. I understand. Living in a community where I know Holocaust survivors and their stories of unimaginable physical and emotional pain, breathing the same air as these survivors in my neighborhood, it becomes complicated or perhaps even insulting to make cliché statements like, "God is always here watching over us and caring for us."

And yet I continue to feel this way not in spite of them but because of them. I draw on their strength, their seemingly beyond human capabilities to live on and bring their spirits to all of us. As one dear friend, whose wife and child were murdered in the concentration camps, told me, "There was one thought that kept me alive every day in the concentration camp. Who would tell the world of this? I was going to survive-I needed to survive to share this with the world." He has. But not in show stopping recounts of horror but rather as a spiritual leader of a synagogue for over forty years. *He has brought his message of his powerful eternal soul back from horror and gave it into the hands of those of us who search for strength and meaning. Even in the midst of pain those spirits can speak of meaning. That is not a human quality, it's a godly one.* Even

Can We Prove This Soul Exists 15

with tragedy, somehow spirituality always seems present for those who want it to be.

Still, I must acknowledge how hard it is for so many of us to really believe or focus energy on our spiritual selves. With the world in such a seeming mess, innocent people suffering, our lives being full of activity... there is plenty pointing us away from believing, away from connecting to our most deepest, purist, alive selves. Anyone can point to times in life that would seem to declare something quite contrary to a genuine spirituality in life. All of us could wonder why there isn't so much more or at least as much that points us toward believing? I've personally searched for proof. If only we had clear proof of God, of some divine parent. Wouldn't a miracle be so wonderful? Anything to brighten our spirits. What's one miracle to an omnipotent God? Yet we know we'd better not depend on it. It's not coming. I mean, you haven't seen it yet. You can't keep relying and basing your life's philosophies on some revelation that might never come.

After all, there hasn't been a really good miracle for so long. You may not believe there were ever really fantastic miracles in the first place.

Yes, I've heard about the big sea splitting a long time ago but couldn't it have been a big tidal wave that was dressed up in emperor's clothing? And so it is with all of those Torah stories, just that, potentially creative stories meant to give hope or as some would say to manipulate and help others gain power and control. Pity. But if they were *real* miracles, if God showed others in earlier generations these show stoppers and made it easy for them to believe then why not lay a couple on us, help the non-believers believe and the believers release their doubts.

Even if you believe in these Torah stories you are still left with profound questions. These miracles in the Torah always seemed followed by some awfully strange, mass confusion on the part of people who saw these convincing miracles. For heavens' sakes, the Jews of the desert who saw it all, ten plagues, splitting sea, manna falling from heaven, hearing the voice of God... proceed to almost immediately create a golden calf for idol worship. I can only imagine that if you or I saw such miracles today we'd never think of such insolence. The world would be a better place. So if He really can do it, anytime would be a great time. Why not do it? In the absence of such miracles people will talk. They'll say it's because there really weren't any miracles- just stories. Where's the beef?

If it's true that God's purpose is to offer us a fulfilling, meaningful life then why give everyone else from the past a leg up. What did we do to deserve this "isolation?" What luck; to be born in this later generation where *blind* faith is the best we have to offer. After endless moments of considering these issues, a simple, obvious answer "dawned" on me.

The Miracle You've Been Waiting For

Imagine with me. Tomorrow morning the sun peaks over the horizon in all of its splendor. Suddenly, something fantastic occurs. The majestic sun rises with unusual vibrating sounds emanating from the heavens as the world hears a thunderous voice scream out in a deep baritone, "Be Good." All of us heard it, unmistakably. Could you imagine how the world would change? Now increase the miracle. Imagine this "voice" continues to speak the same words every morning at the split second that the sun starts our day wherever you may be in the world. How incredible. How the world would be a different place. Years later, there'd be love everywhere, no more wars, armies would be disbanded, complete belief in God, unity, prioritization of the important things in life-our families above all, genuine sensitivity, such sacrificing to help others, no more selfishness. What a beautiful world this would be.

Can We Prove This Soul Exists

Do you believe it? Oh, how I'd sleep better at night believing it but it's unfortunately light years away from the truth. My prediction would be a different reality. After years of a heavenly voice commanding or pleading with us to "Be Good" we'd have the same exact world we have today. But what about the "voice" you ask? How could people avoid the "voice?" The very proof of godliness, that something real, divine and deeper exists. After all, what greater proof can you have than God speaking to you every single day at sunrise? Naturally, at first everyone would be focusing on the voice but sooner than later the "theories" would develop. Here are four of the most popular ones.

Theory #1. God is alive and well and has graced us with a crystal clear presence.

Theory #2. The "voice" is the voice of aliens. We must create new research to understand the delivery system of this message so that we can communicate with these other beings.

Theory #3. The galaxy is constantly expanding and as it does new matter has leaked into the atmosphere and the "voice" is merely new examples of thunderous gaseous matter that is burning off due to the rising sun. Don't flatter yourself. Like a newborn baby who smiles at you, it's just gas. In fact, scientists have recreated these sounds in a laboratory manipulating similar gases to explode and say things sounding remarkably like "p'ease pudding hot" and "find it at Sears."

Theory #4. It is proof of God. He exists. However, He only concerns Himself with this world precisely at sunrise. After all, if He was really connected to us all day and night then why doesn't He talk to us at noon, dinnertime and midnight? This theory persuades people to rise with the sun (called Sunnies), do something kind and then do whatever they desire with the rest of their lives because God ain't looking or maybe, poor chap, He can't see us after sunrise.

And of course the list would go on. *Simply put, miracles are not the Godly proof that changes behavior long term nor do they seem to even prove spirituality.* This is the lesson taught by the Jews in the desert as they consistently acted out of anything but faith; creating idols and complaining regularly about their situation causing them to be punished by wandering and dying in the desert for 40 years, even after seeing unusual miracle after unusual miracle. No, the show of miracles has little to do with changing the essence of who we are. *Our belief has only to do with how much of the show we wish to perceive. Our world is full of miracles. The question is if you and I are seeing the miracles and allowing them to bring us to greater heights of inner peace.* Isn't there something divine already speaking to us in many ways? When the sun peaks over the horizon why do I need God to say "Be good" or "Find it at Sears?" He already has said good morning with one of the most breathtaking messages known to us: sunrise. Its splendor cannot be matched or copied. Can either of us go on listing every miracle of our world? *Everything is a miracle if you choose to see deeper than others or than you have before.* Your body, mind, emotions, ability to give life, plant a simple seed and grow a flower, love, hate; isn't all of it quite miraculous regardless of any explanations surrounding them?

Perhaps all of these "miracles" are nothing more than scientific functions for you. "C'mon," you'll say, "science can explain it so there is nothing miraculous about it." But why does science detract from our internal vision and sense of spirituality? Remember the old story of the man who is sitting on top of his house during a horrible flood? As the waters rise around him a little motor boat comes his way and a rescue worker urges him to get in before he drowns.

"No need," he says, "God will save me."

The boat leaves and returns an hour later after removing some others from the neighborhood.

Once again, the driver of the boat tells the man to get in.

"Really not necessary. God will save me."

An hour later the boat returns for its final attempt. The driver explains that he must move on to the next community to save others and this is the last chance the person has for safety. But his pleading isn't heard.

"I've told you, no need to help me. God will save me."

And with that the rescue worker moved on. Within an hour the man drowns. He enters heaven and lets it be known that he is rather perplexed and quite upset.

"God, I trusted in You. How could you let me die when I believed in you? Why didn't you help me?"

To which God replies angrily, "Help you? For heaven's sake, I sent you a boat three times and you wouldn't get in!"

If God gives us a miracle then how should He do it? Science only means that there is a rational delivery system to the miracles around us. Would you prefer that there were no scientific explanations for everything that goes on around us? That would be quite depressing because it would diminish you and me to an infant like status. We would have no consistency or realistic expectations. If there were no consistent delivery system explainable by science you'd be planting watermelon seeds only to grow watermelons this season, grapefruits the next season and perhaps shoes the following one. Gravitational forces would be pulling individuals at different rates putting the diet industry out of business. Every part of our lives would be severely disrupted. We'd go insane and be reduced to vicious animals. Life would be impossible for us if there were no rhyme or reason to any of it. If everything was a miracle defined by lack of its scientific explanation and consistency we could not navigate our world. We'd end up simply waiting around for God to perform for us much the way a child must simply give in to the knowledge that the adults in his world must supply life for him. *How gracious of Divine nature to offer genuine miracles that are yet predictable so that we can become a part of them and cause these miracles to happen. It's an ultimate kindness to offer us this partnership much the way a parent must give to a child in a way that allows that child to have self-respect. The child must believe she is an integral part of the system and that she has a place is causing goodness. Otherwise she will be nothing more than a dependant individual who lacks the skills to give to herself or others.* Don't get thrown off your desire to grow as a spiritual being and *see the fire. Science is a loving gift that entitles us to predict and understand our surroundings so that we can become working partners in this family of life called nature.*

Scientific Conundrums

And yet we are still offered just enough scientific inconsistency to help us recognize that there is some other miraculous force at the heart of it all demanding that we realize we'll never be in perfect control of nature's miracles. All planting doesn't lead to growing, all sex doesn't lead to pregnancy, all love doesn't lead to happiness, all clouds don't lead to rain and so on. We are not in charge even if science seems to want to believe that it has every explanation. If you still would like to increase your faith by finding natural miracles that science admits it cannot explain, you're in luck. We are assisted in our belief through unexplainable parts of our world, godly magic that confounds science. But as a blessing for us, these areas are ones that don't immediately affect our ability to navigate our world. They are mysterious pieces of our unexplained universe that point to godliness without disrupting our daily order.

Can We Prove This Soul Exists 27

My favorite is the speed of light. Light travels at 299,792.5 kilometers per second (approximately 300 million meters per second) whether or not the source of the light or the observer of the light is moving! To add to the confusion, the same light beam behaves like a wave when measured one way and behaves like a particle when measured another way. Science has miraculously been able to study the speed of light and discovered these fascinating miracles. To understand this miracle I was given this example. Pretend for a moment that you are being pitched to by famous Hall of Famer Nolan Ryan. Nolan could throw 100 miles per hour pitches somewhat consistently. If you decided to start running at Nolan's 100 mph pitched ball it would reach you faster, right? For example, if you started running at 10 mph at his 100 mph pitch, then the ball would be traveling toward you at 110 mph and would obviously reach you faster than if you stayed at the plate and didn't run toward the pitch at all. Makes sense? Of course it does except for the fact that this is not true of light. Scientific data has proven that light doesn't reach the object any faster even if the object is racing toward the light. Am I making sense? No. But that's miracles for you sometimes. They don't always do exactly what you think they'll do. Now add a beautiful ingredient to this paradigm. What were the first words recorded as spoken by God? "Let there be light." No doubt that the sun and all forms of light are a powerful, both a healing and destructive force. But it also has unexplainable properties. *"Let there be light," indeed. A miracle – something scientists cannot explain-something that goes against our brilliant logical theories-and it is a powerful force every second of every moment of our entire lives.*

We will always have to ultimately rely on our spiritual selves to truly navigate life. Only our spirituality, our immortal essence is in our ultimate and absolute control.

Much like listening to and studying a love interest, it is for each of us to develop a relationship with the parts of the world around us that we are taken with or feel a need to know. As we work at understanding it we develop ourselves, becoming an integral part of nature around us.

The Simple Way to Finding God

God wants to give to us through his miraculous delivery system. For example, He offers us water, the very essence of our body and world. What does He do? He sends it to us from the sky. Usually, it's not too complicated; don't have to work hard to create it. It just falls. Now, how do you want it to fall? By some unexplained reason? Whichever way it's administered, we'll explain it even though we could never control it or recreate it. Rain falls and we are bound by it, unable to manipulate it. How beautiful. What an immeasurable gift. Like a parent who loves a child so deeply that sometimes that parent just wants to give unequivocally to the child without lesson, rain finds its way to us; a simple, magical connection to our own spirits. But what is the common reaction to rain? This spiritual treasure trove is ignored for comments like, "Darn, I wanted to barbecue. Where's an umbrella when I need one?" Have you ever sat back and stared at the rain, I mean really opened your eyes wide and said aloud "how beautiful"-smelled its moist innocence, literally spoken to the rain and gracefully thanked it for giving to you, for feeding your plants and your world? How wonderful this gift of rain, satisfying my thirst and hunger, nourishing my seeds and leaves, cleaning my air. I feel so connected to my spirit to see God giving me life enhancing, pure rain. I've even stood outside in the rain purposely to feel it-to allow myself to be absorbed in it. Only recently did I read with my children about the rain. I learned what you probably know-that our water here on earth is vaporized by the heat causing it to rise above (it's lighter than oxygen at that point) and as it hits the sky the cold air causes the steam to turn back into solid water forming a cloud which will then rain water on us all over again. When I shared this with a friend, she said, "It's like the water is breathing." I found that simply beautiful and thanked her for giving me a part of her unique connection to rainwater. I will forever smile with a new dimension of life every time I see rain or any water at all. *My world is "breathing" around me and I want, I must be a part of that endless source of living.* Perhaps you don't feel much of anything in your soul and yet you could. And so it is with everything in your world. *The ability to lead a spiritual, fulfilling life lies completely within you, not God.* He's given you a world full of miracles and signs and is regularly communicating with you. The only question you want to ask yourself is: *Am I listening with spiritual ears and watching with spiritual eyes?* My journey is about finding my way *within*-it's all in me ready to be nurtured and grown along with the splendor of life. I don't need to be a rabbi, priest or spiritual guru. Each of us has godliness within us. Rain watching is just one example of finding your way to your inner self. *Each of us is an integral part of developing this world. Our uniqueness is expressed with every interest we have and choice we make. No one else will feel and think exactly like you. No one else can do for this world exactly what you could. Science is here to help us take part and develop nature. Every consistent pattern of life begs us to study it and bring our unique godliness to it.*

Your Unique Gift

When you see the fire around you, not only does the world become a feast of fantastic pictures but you can't help but to begin to indulge in taking part. With this attitude you can plant a seed and become an everlasting part of the spiritual miracles of life. No matter what you do, you can become a part of this immortal life that connects you to your inner spirit. Until you experience this, you'll never notice what you're missing. You might be thinking, "Plant a flower? That's it?" I understand that simple actions are done everyday. But anyone can see that sometimes an action of love can be incredibly meaningful and other times we can merely be going through the motions: giving your child a hug, discussing your thoughts with your lover, doing a simple kindness for another-all actions that are done often with meaning and too often with little meaning. How much meaning do you want to bring to your actions, love and life? Can't you fit much more meaning into your everyday? All of us can. *The specific question you want to ask yourself is what's the unique part of you that you want to bring to this world?* Everything you do in a day can be done with a powerful force of instant connection to a part of you and the world you may have been largely missing. You smile kindly at someone, hold your child's hand, walk your pet, think of your lover, calm someone at work… anything can become about attaining a greater sense of spirituality if you want it to. You don't need to visit a mountaintop, study for ten years, start a divinity degree in order to tap into the godliness you have within. *You can live the spiritual life everyday just where you are - because that's where spirituality and miracles are- within you.*

Your unique gift is what gives our world and every person such great potential. Each of us is so completely different because godliness is infinite and offers every single person a completely different spirit much the way we can have different fingerprints and DNA. *When each of us follows our heart we bring out new things in this world that no one else could have discovered in the same way.* That new music, painting, scientific theory, recipe, joke, invention, way to express love is something only you could bring to this world in that exact way. *The world will forever be different, fuller because of what you brought to it.* Whether the "whole world" will ever know about it or it will remain just in your family is irrelevant. It is still something you've "connected with" and brought out in this world. Suddenly, you've made yourself uniquely infinite. You've become a part of creating this world. It simply would be a different place if you weren't in it. *The fact is that you and I can* mean *something and change this world-now that's miraculous and a taste of godliness. Follow your heart. Whatever naturally sings to you is your inner spirit trying to lead you to your place in this world, a place where you can add something and make a difference.* The most inspirational stories tend to be those of people who use every ounce of energy to live for what they believe in, to forward a goal no matter how important or unimportant it may seem to the world.

A person who overcomes all odds like Lance Armstrong, the American who won five (maybe more in the future) straight Tour De France titles less than 3 years after being diagnosed with advanced testicular cancer that spread to his lungs and brain, was given a 40 percent chance of survival, underwent brain surgery, testes surgery and chemotherapy inspires us because we love his determination to "be." I don't know that winning a bicycle race is godly or has much importance to the world. It doesn't carry much meaning for me personally but that's what's so magical about each of us. To Lance Armstrong it can be magical and spiritual if he allows it to be. His unique desire to rise to this challenge could represent his personal godliness. He has sung his song, found his way to "be," given voice to his inner spirit and expressed it in his own way. The rest of us can choose to hear this voice or not but can never take away how he has changed his world and any other world of someone who has drawn strength from his perseverance.

My first thought was I was going to die. I didn't think, well God, I'm going to be a better bike rider, a better person, I'm going to be stronger, I'm going to be happier. I didn't think about any of that but that's what happened.

Lance Armstrong

Beethoven wrote music as a deaf man. He was drawn to communicate in his unique way. Vincent Van Gogh had a burning desire to express himself. I don't know if he felt spiritual through his expression but I can when I stare into his paintings of desire and sadness. He killed himself as a young man without ever selling a single painting but only after he changed our world. He didn't give himself a chance to see what his art could do for the world but his unique soul was articulated. Helen Keller proved to humanity that some of the most wonderful, wise people are waiting in silence to speak to us.

I thank God for my handicaps, for through them I have found myself, my work and God.

Helen Keller

You may never listen to Beethoven, look into the Starry Night, enter a bicycle race or read Keller's poetry but the ingredients of this world have changed because of them. *And so every day you and I can change the world with our unique expression.* Don't hold it in and wait for the right time. Follow your dreams in some way no matter how small it may seem. You don't have to be a Beethoven, Van Gogh, Keller, or Armstrong to change the world. You don't have to be remembered by an hour long memoir of your life on the Biography channel to have made a difference. Something small yet meaningful to you can make a difference in so many lives.

♦ *Exercise* ♦

1.   List five people who have made an important difference in your life in a personal way.

2.   List the names of five people whose lives you'd like to make a difference to.

3.   Add five things you'd like to do or already do in a special way that others couldn't quite do the same. (For example, you can give love to someone that could never be as meaningful if that love came from someone else).

4.   Add one thing you've been wishing to do that can make even the slightest difference in another's life or serve as a personal inspiration to yourself.

5.   Now do it. Stop worrying about how it will look or whether or not you'll be successful. The fantastic thing about partnering with God is that you only do your part and God will do the rest. You can't *make* anything happen. You can only set things into motion, put forth an idea, build a logical system. Then it is your godly

partner's decision as to whether you will have the success you desired. We can't plan with such extreme boundaries because that would imply that we are completely in charge. That thought isolates us and has little concern for others. We want to go forward in partnership with godliness, knowing that ultimately when we are genuinely spiritual our paths lead us to even greater spirituality that was beyond our "plan."

Naturally, there is this balance in any partnership that takes time to develop. I can't sit around waiting for fate to knock on my door and yet I can't create such a strict vision that I won't be able to see the signs when God would like me to take a different direction. My career is somewhat typical (it could even be seen as comical) of how this symbiotic relationship with God can work.

Since eleven years old, I've wanted to be a rabbi (my first planned career was veterinary medicine but I became a bit of a philosopher so my dreams changed). In fact, the only reason I completed my graduate degree in counseling was to make myself a better rabbi. I had started a limited private psychology practice while waiting to complete my rabbinical degree. I then landed a wonderful position as a rabbi. My dream had come true. My parents were very proud and my wife felt strong in her commitment to our collective goal to help others. I was going to make a difference and God must've brought me to this fabulous moment. The stars were aligned and my life was developing just as planned. Yet, it was only a short six months until I realized I had made a huge mistake becoming a rabbi; a lifetime of planning reversed by six months. I learned that my plan stunk. It took me another six months to realize that I wasn't going to be able to turn my sadness around. Exactly one year from fulfilling my life's dream of becoming a rabbi, I resigned and found myself working as a counselor in the Miami family court for $20,000 (less than half of what I had made as a rabbi) plus added income through my budding private practice. But because I was a partner in creation and running this world, I took the changes in stride. See, I reminded myself that my dream wasn't to be a rabbi. My real dream was to help others and I had deemed the rabbinate as my best venue. When that wasn't working for me I knew I had to find a new venue. Working in the Family Court system helped me see the plight and awful struggle of children of divorce, people I've happily dedicated my life to helping. I never would have found myself there without my own career struggles. I like to think God wanted me to offer these children help, that somehow I had a unique way of helping that convinced God to put me on the task. Had I been successful as a rabbi-my lifelong dream-I would've never helped children of divorce-the accomplishment that I consider at this moment as my greatest professional achievement.

It simply wasn't up to me. I offered God my vision of helping and He offered me a plan. I will always be a partner with God. I'm going to fit into His plans and see what else I can do for the system. I love being a part of a family, a community, a team. My work has to not only fit into my life plans but into the plans for every other human being and nature as a whole. That's a great deal of people to keep in mind and God has quite a task keeping everyone's lives interacting while helping each individual develop his and her spirituality and potential. (My small mind envisions it as some intricate Scrabble board where every word depends on a letter from another word.)

Everything happens for a reason. *You just need to search for the fire and feel its warmth more and more.*

Responsibility
Being partner does demand a certain sense of responsibility. An employee doesn't have to answer to others about the big issues of success. An employee can apologize and say, "I'm sorry I didn't accomplish my task but I tried my best." *A partner has to answer about the bottom line, completing*

tasks. "I tried," doesn't cut it. As partners with God, we can't shrug and say, "It's all up to God." Even though we must defer to God, we still have to sense what He wants from us and then complete our task. We can't just *try*. This is our world, our place, our home and once we've discovered our dreams we have to follow them.

Follow the Dreams that are Worth Dreaming

You may be thinking that dreams are larger than life and you can't spend your time chasing dreams. It's not about the big things. This is a crucial part of my message and connection to you. With every kiss of your loved one, every moment to help another, every second to plant a seed, you are adding /developing/partnering and yes perhaps following a dream.

Dreams are what we make of them. Every person should have loads of dreams and they should be soulful dreams. You have to consider what your

Follow the Dreams Worth Dreaming 45

many dreams are and why you have the dreams that you do. Many people dream of having huge amounts of money rained upon them and unfortunately, the dream is attached to a selfish desire to purchase things and get noticed-leading to bliss, of course. How many people dream of money with their primary goal of using that money to start a charity or help others in some way? Why aren't our main dreams full of having a loving family, raising children who care for others, loving our parents?

Our dreams have been confused for responses to low self-esteem and lack of meaning. People dream of becoming a movie star or sports hero. How many stories do you hear concerning this group that imply they are leading lives of bliss? How many of these movie stars have never been divorce, are happily married, close with their children and have never used drugs? You can sense that there aren't too many because the stories of those Hollywood stars who are married thirty years or more stand out in our minds. But people want to be like them because somehow, having the ability to purchase expensive items, pay to be pampered and have people recognize and intrude in your life to the extent that you have no privacy is far more appealing than being unknown to the world but the most loving, important person to your own spouse and child. These meaningless dreams serve to make dreamers feel terrible about themselves. I'm not the rich one, the famous one, the sports legend. These are not dreams. They're social brainwashing. People mistake a "dream" for a "has it all without much work" story. *The American dream was never meant to be a get rich quick scheme. It was the beautiful dream of being able to develop a life for oneself; the ability to love who we wanted, pray to who we wanted and yes, have the ability to have as fair a chance to work hard and be rewarded financially as anyone else. Dreaming is about connecting to your inner soul and feeling what is special about you. Follow that dream and your partnership with God will always be a solid one.*

Not Enough Time?

Perhaps you're thinking that you're stretched so many different ways that the thought of following a dream is akin to sprouting wings and flying. Between your job and kids, it's all you can do to stay awake past 9 p.m. We have a fantastic way of being busy. We have a magical way of *thinking* we're busy. We are the busiest people ever. We are so busy, we have no time for our kids or ourselves. But we have time to "veg out." The vegging out is our reward for being so busy. It's a must, like exercise, breathing, eating, and loving. I believe in time for oneself but how that became translated to blindly watching television and other such mindless pursuits is beyond me. Why can't time for self be about writing a poem, drawing a picture, praying or meditating, having a catch or having a pretend tea party with "Barbie" and your kid, hearing an interesting lecture, making love with your spouse or reading a book or newspaper? The average American vegges out by watching 1,460 hours per year of television. We sure think we're busy. I'm not saying that television doesn't have its value but very little of it will add meaning to your life when compared to other meaningful pursuits. Now there are hundreds of channels to keep anyone "busy." Learn to follow little dreams. Learn to spend time with loved ones pursuing meaningful moments. Imagine visiting hospital patients with your spouse or kids weekly. Imagine volunteering one hour a week at any shelter. Imagine how much dream pursuing you can manage when the dreams you chase are ones that build your soul-the very heart of your self-esteem

Finding Your Soul

No one could possibly outline every part of spirituality as though it was some shopping list as it's incredibly unique. At the risk of repeating myself, my message is simply that spirituality is abound-it's everywhere and we'll talk more about

Finding Your Soul 49

finding it. But first, believe me when I tell you, it's everywhere. Wherever you want to find it is where it will always be-In your lover's touch, in the angelic face of your sleeping or smiling child, in the bird singing above you, in the leaves that reach out to you, in the coincidences that drew you to meaningful relationships, in the eyes of that adoring pet, in the sudden great ideas you have, in the deep love in your heart that can both lift you and scare you. You don't have to travel the earth to find it. *Travel only into your heart and soul and then spirituality will be eternally yours. Once you begin, there's no stopping you. There's a reason for everything in your life. You just have to be open to seeing those reasons. Spirituality leads you as much as you want it to. Your experiences can be drawn on your spirit, everything that comes your way has a divine purpose. You become a part of it when you meet this challenge to connect with your soul. As you begin to focus on the fire in and around you the world begins to make sense. Everywhere you turn, it's there.*

The great partnership that we are offered in the ongoing creation of this world comes with our ability to focus our energy toward our eternal selves. Each of us has to discover for ourselves, involve ourselves in those things that invite spirituality into our lives. It's a *partnership*. We don't just sit here and wait for Divine inspiration to come upon us. We start the process by doing things that speak to our spirits. Not long ago, a relative was complaining to me about her life. There was no man in it and until she was married and with a family, there was to be no happiness in her life. I respected her for feeling that her happiness in life was to be greatly experienced through developing her own family. But I took issue with her complacency in this holding pattern that didn't allow her to develop until she fell in love. I told her what I'm telling you. Life is too precious to wait and our spirit needs to be constantly nurtured. I asked her to involve herself in meaningful pursuits. In her case, if she was missing a sense of connection, perhaps she needed to do something that drew her closer to others. She tried many things but it was the pediatric oncology floor where she felt herself grow. Suddenly life wasn't about waiting but living. It was two years later, which would have felt like a decade had she not begun to live and give, when she finally found her soulmate, at a function surrounding kids with terminal illnesses-a function she never would have attended had it not been for her meaningful giving. All we have to do is start the process and God leads us where we are needed. None of us can dictate our lives. That wouldn't be a partnership. Nor can we wait for fate to knock on our door. Tapping into our inner spirit is about a balance between our personal meaningful interests while being flexible enough to see the fire and be lead forward where we need to go.

How many things would you love to do but don't because you tell yourself there is no time, you don't have the energy, or it's just plain silly? How many meaningful things could you do for others but don't? How many hugs and warm glances have your loved ones missed out on? How many smiles haven't happened yet that could because of you?

A friend of mine told me that the day his son turned 18, he and his son went together to give blood. He imparted to his son a meaningful definition of adulthood, greater flexibility in being able to make a difference. How can you begin to make the slightest difference? Everyone can and must if they want to live in a spiritual partnership. It's not our job to decide what the world needs. Rather, we have to see our own fire, feel what speaks to us. That will lead us to offering our fullest potential to this world. Don't think about where you'll end up. Live today and begin your partnership with an action, whether physical or verbal, that will give you a sense of meaning if only for a moment. It doesn't have to be a grand gesture. Let it be a simple hug given or a phone call to inquire of a friend, a walk at sunrise, stopping to help an old lady across the street-anything that you are doing with the purpose of seeing the fire one day. The more you involve yourself with spiritual gestures, the more fire you'll see and the greater Divine paths, inspirations and "coincidences" will follow you. What you can offer, I never will and visa versa. We're drawn on different spirits and as such are meant to bring different things to the world.

Moses shows us this message of uniqueness well with his modesty. As he leads the Jewish people out of Egypt and into the desert, he is referred to as the most humble of men. Unless humility is some form of reality twisting, it's hard to understand how this spiritual giant who God regularly conversed with as though some younger sibling could possibly be humble. I'd imagine that Moses must have clearly seen that he was undeniably holier than others. But he recognized that others are unique and he didn't have what they had. Imagine if you were a leading gem collector. Even though you may have the most precious collection of gems, you would still be humbled by the fact that another collector had perhaps the most beautiful single gemstone in the world. Moses had to have known he was one of the holiest men in history. But he understood that every person has a unique spirit that gives each of us the ability to bring out spirituality in a way that no one else can. He knew he made a difference but his humility was born out of the knowledge that he could never make the difference that someone else could in his or her own way.

If God is my partner, why doesn't God simply give me everything I want?
In any meaningful relationship it takes two people to search in order to learn about their friendship. To genuinely know your spouse, for example, you need to be in regular contact about many parts of life. At the very least you need to

talk, spend quiet time, laugh and work together on developing your life goals. You learn about your spouse from every interaction, every moment and gesture, all of it brings you to better understand the deeper part of your spouse. It isn't enough to only discuss the bills or laugh at a comedy club or have deep talks about life. The most loving relationships do all of that and then some. These spouses know that they learn about each other from every interaction, from discussing politics, philosophy, and dreams to holding each other when one is sad and cheering when one is happy. The spousal relationship demands continuous contact and commitment to giving and receiving.

If my relationship is primarily about what I can receive from my spouse, then I will quickly lose my ability to genuinely love my spouse. I will no longer search to love her but will become satiated taking what she loves to give. I won't try to learn more about her or find greater ways to love or understand her. I will be busy taking and taking and become enveloped in a selfish role.

It is far too easy for any person to become intoxicated with being given to, losing sight that there is deeper love found in a reciprocal relationship. It is when I recognize that my spouse is not there only to give to me but to receive from me as well that I am moved to learn more about her- how I can give to her and love her. In the process she will learn more meaningful ways to give to me because our relationship will no longer be reduced to "gifts" but to a connection and sharing that touches deeper that mere receiving. The closer we become the more we will learn about each other. As we learn more we increase our ability to give more.

If the relationship is mainly surrounding her giving, even her ability to give to me in a deeper way is severely diminished. She can only offer me gifts- items and gestures that can never offer me deep connections because I don't share enough of myself for her to know me deeply. All of her giving would be distanced by our lack of connection.

True love lasts because we can touch each other on a deep level that only comes through the give and take relationship. Once there is true love, new meaning is added to every kind gesture. Consider the difference between my wife making dinner when I've had a hard day and making me the same dinner after offering me an empathic hug. The dinner satisfies a real need regardless, it's a physical gift. But the hug only becomes meaningful because we connect and feel an oneness in that hug. The hug is stale if I simply receive it and don't manage to offer it back. The oneness in that hug comes from my giving as much as my receiving. She can only know how and when to hug me because I offer myself, my own desire to make her happy. When that hug is full of meaning, the dinner then changes too. It's no longer about satisfying needs. The dinner becomes a metaphoric hug, a desire to share and do for each other as a gesture of a loving connection.

There are those spouses who are too giving from the start of the relationship. Their spouses find it too easy to be so taken with the goodness they receive that there is little reciprocity. This imbalance is devastating to a relationship. If I were their marriage counselor, the first thing I'd suggest to such a couple would be for that giving spouse to stop giving so much. The receiving spouse doesn't have a chance to find a way to love the giver, know the simpler and deeper desires and needs of the giver. This concept applies to every meaningful relationship.

Imagine the parent who is extremely financially giving. If Dad becomes the ATM machine, his children never get the chance to search for other meaningful ways he can be helpful or close to them. He puts himself into a one dimensional role. He may think he's simply showing love but if every chance he has he overwhelms his kids with money, those kids will see Dad as the "money giver." His loving nature, advice, emotional support will all be diminished. Children as well as adults enjoy receiving and too often our immature nature thinks the perfect relationship would be one where all we have to do is receive and not give. That parent has to stop giving money and force his kids to relate to him in some other way. He has to allow them the space to search his goodness out and find other ways to connect instead of merely taking the money and running. Once the money stops, his children will be forced to find new ways to truly connect and relate to Dad.

The extraordinary message that God sends us daily is that He wants to actually have a relationship with us! He wants to connect with us and have us learn about each other. If He merely gives us what we want when we want it, He will quickly be relegated to Daddy War Bucks status. We'd stop thinking about relating to Him and just take our blessings and run. *But He doesn't just give us what we want. Instead He asks us to relate to Him, consider all the ways we can find Him, love Him, talk to Him, draw strength from Him. He can be like our parent and like our spouse and like our sibling.* But He can't be any of that if He's an ATM machine.

The proof that this one way giving relationship doesn't work comes from the experience that the Jews had with God in the desert. They had been miraculously saved and brought out of slavery from Egypt into an empty desert. The Jews were truly in a stage of infancy after 210 years of harsh and cruel enslavement. God saw it fit to treat them as infants and give them everything they needed without question. A food substance fell from the sky called manna which Judaic commentary explains could taste however the consumer wanted it to. A well of water traveled alongside them which again took on the flavor of the consumer's imagination. Commentaries even describe miracles surrounding their clothing never soiling and even growing with them if they were children still developing. Yes, they had to keep certain laws, pick up camp and move at the drop of a hat when God decided and continue to learn more about their God and personal godliness. But for the most part blessings literally rained down upon them. What was their response? Rather obnoxious at times. Although of course there are deeper explanations to these biblical stories, their complaints are recorded in a tone of spoiled children. When they don't have water they complain as if it's God's *job* to constantly quench their thirst. They complain about a lack of meat even though they receive manna which could taste like meat if they desired.

The list of immature actions go on and on culminating in serving an idol in the golden calf when Moses is seemingly delayed one day from his return from the top of Mt. Sinai. They become hysterical at the thought that Moses could be dead leaving them leaderless and look only to satisfy their childish fears instead of concerning themselves with the connection, the relationship to God and considering various options. They diminish themselves to whining adolescents who need to be taught a lesson no different than today's overindulgent parent who reminds his teen that the world doesn't revolve around him. We tell our teens that they must begin to see outside themselves and yes, even consider what they can do for their parents to bring meaning to the relationship. I believe God knew that this treatment would lead to this horrendous outcome but He needed to show them (and you and me) at the start of their nationhood that this ATM machine giving never leads to a rich relationship.

We are given opportunities beyond belief to relate to our godliness within. Finding your unique road to godliness and this partnership is your responsibility to yourself and your partner. That's why you must find your own way. If you and I believe that you are unique then I can't begin to create a list of things that'll definitely work for you. I can only describe a world that is waiting for you- and no one else but you to add to it immeasurably in a way no one else can.

Another reason God can't give us everything we want is that He has to view the greater picture. He's responsible for the entire company whereas you and I are only the VP's in charge of our part of the business. We might see advancement for our part of the business but that might not work for the entire company. I've wanted my books, for example, to hit the market at certain times but my publisher has to consider if there is another book in the same genre that is already slated for that time. They don't say to me that my idea is a bad one for my book. They do say it might be a great idea but they have their entire book list to consider and I have to respect their greater goal. The partnership isn't 50/50 simply because we haven't been given the ability to completely see what God will always see. But we have been chosen to continue to create this world together. You and I continue to try and if we're listening with spiritual ears, we'll see the fire and be taken to our place, our own corner office, in our own unique destiny.

Acting Like a Partner

As a partner, we are expected to act in ways that we would never consider. Too often, God is seen as Omnipotent, basically so awesome that He can't be related to. Then there is the disaster of people who imply that they are the only ones that can relate to God and they will tell you what to do and you are expected to just do it, no questions asked. But as you allow yourself to *feel* like you have a relationship/partnership with God, things change quickly. It's no longer His world. *It is our world and we have a responsibility to develop its godliness.* What is amazing is that we, you and I, can actually change how God plans to manage the world. *Today can be totally different for you and the world because you want it to be. This is the start of your miraculous powers.* In fact God demands that you relate to Him and indicate the way you think things should be.

In the Torah, we get to hear what God is thinking. When angels are sent to Abraham, one of them is to continue on to destroy the evil people of Sodom and Amorrah. But God begins to question Himself as to whether or not He should share this upcoming event with Abraham.

God says, "How can I do this and not tell Abraham? After all, he is going to follow my commands and instruct his children to love me."

God is describing to us this wonderful concept of partnership and family that we share with Him. He feels he has an *obligation* to notify Abraham of His intentions. If Abraham is His partner, then he has a right to know about anything that will affect his ability to carry out his job.

Abraham responds as a full partner and family member when he tries to save Sodom and Amorrah. The Torah tells us these towns were full of cruel, narcissistic people. God relates to Abraham through an angel that He plans to destroy these cities. Now what would you or I do under those circumstances? I tell you what I wouldn't do. I wouldn't begin to argue with God. I'd figure who am I to have any say in this? If God has justly decided that these people deserve death then to suggest something different would be insulting to God. It would be as if to say, "Maybe you're mistaken God. Are you *sure* these people deserve this? Perhaps you want to review your notes again." If God is just and omnipotent then there really isn't much to say. But Abraham is anything but silent. He is downright pushy. He questions God's judgment. "Is it right to kill innocent among the guilty?" Abraham convinces God to make a deal: if he can find 50 righteous people then God won't destroy the towns. What becomes more seemingly absurd is that when Abraham visits these towns and can't find 50 righteous people he renegotiates his deal with God five times, each round reducing the number of righteous people he needs to find. As the story progresses, the town is destroyed because he can't find enough (if any) righteous people.

What is outlined in this story is the first successful partnership between God and a human being. Abraham takes a stand attempting to change the way God plans to treat *our* world. God obviously has created us to work together in some fashion and that is why Abraham steps up to the plate. He understands that he has a job here. The world does not only belong to God even though God has the final word. It belongs to us all and God wants to know from Abraham what he thinks and how he might determine how to run the world. As you look closer at the story you begin to see Abraham's argument.

Abraham sees himself as God's PR man. His role, like everyone else's, is to help bring godliness to the world. He wants to help others see their unique connection to godliness and have a seat on the Board of the World. He argues that if these towns are destroyed, people will begin to say, "Some God you have, killing innocent with the guilty. You call that justice?" Abraham doesn't dare say that God is not just. He knows that if God plans something it is right even if Abraham can't understand it. But Abraham must consider the people he works with to help see the godliness. To these people his discussion to have them believe in their unique soul is going to be marred by this impending destruction. They'll find fault with God and not want to listen to Abraham get started about his God.

Consider a PR person. His client might feel that he must do something. But the PR person has to consider how the constituency will perceive it. That PR person's responsibility is to reflect back to the person how his actions will be seen. That person might change his actions in part or completely if the PR person convinces him that it'll hurt his image. That PR person carries a great deal of clout. He's saying, "Look, you want me to have people buy into your message. So you can't do things that I feel are going to make it close to impossible for me to do my job. If you don't consider what I'm saying then I can't do my job and I'm leaving."

If God wants Abraham to be His PR man then He better listen to Abraham's points. Abraham has to say what will help and hurt his ability to have people buy into the God message. True justice becomes less relevant than Abraham's unique ability to help others see the fire. So Abraham says these people won't give me the time of day if they see you as a God that kills what they *perceive* as innocent people. If I can find enough innocent people that would bolster this argument then please reconsider you plan. God is okay with this because He has great respect for His VP in charge of PR. He knows that Abraham isn't selfish and doing this for some kind of ego trip (I got God to change His mind). He acted with the purest of intentions, considering how his ability to bring godliness to the masses might be affected. God doesn't tell Abraham how to do his business. Perhaps Abraham could've made a change in his pitch to convince people of godliness even with the destruction of these cities. But God knew that Abraham must've already considered this but concluded that if there were righteous men killed, his ability to convince others would be severely damaged. *God listens and is willing to change His mind and act differently. Miraculous.*

Abraham begins with the number 50 figuring by his own calculations that many people would be disturbed to have so many seemingly innocent people killed under such circumstances. He then moves to lower and lower numbers recognizing that if there were only handfuls of seemingly righteous people who were killed, he'd have fewer people who would be dismayed by such destruction considering how awful everyone knew these towns were. Finally, Abraham stops at nine recognizing that if there are but a handful of seemingly righteous people that are destroyed that won't hurt his PR enough to request God change his plan.

What Abraham does not do is say, "Even if there is one righteous person how can you do this?" because he is never questioning God's justice and decision making. He is only reflecting about how God's actions will affect his ability to help others let God into their lives. If there are so few people who seem righteous then Abraham will be able to help others understand that perhaps these people were not as righteous as they thought considering they chose to live in such cruel surroundings. If there are 50 righteous people then the argument could be made that they lived in a nasty place because they had enough of a good spirited community of people with which to connect. Again, Abraham wasn't considering whether or not these people deserved to die. They did or else God would never have intended to kill them. But Abraham has to consider all of the different arguments people might give him as to why they'd rather not have much to do with

God. In the end, Abraham's negotiation doesn't change the plans for the two towns but it changes humankind's relationship with God forever.

Successful Negotiations

One instance where a human being negotiated and successfully changed the course of history (and there are many in the Torah-we'll discuss some of them) is when Moses saved the Jewish people. God wanted to destroy the Jewish people in the desert because of their complaints and idol worship of the golden calf. God tells Moses that He will develop a new nation and Moses will be the sole progenitor of this nation. Moses does not act in his own egotistical interest of starting his own nation from scratch and being its only patriarch. Instead he responds as any genuinely good hearted partner would. He describes to God the reaction of the world if the Jews were destroyed in the desert. He explains that he fears people will say that God was strong enough to free the Jews from slavery in

Egypt but not strong enough to lead them to and conquer Israel. This would of course detract from God's glory and the man in the street's ability to want to get close to God. Due solely to this point, God changes His mind and let's the Jews live! Moses never questions God's judgment. He doesn't say, "C'mon, the Jews don't deserve to die. Why not give them another chance." He recognizes God's justice and truth. He doesn't give some empty personal argument like, "I feel bad for them so let them live." He describes with clarity how this action will affect others and his personal ability to be involved with godliness.

This unique partnership is our goal. In order to attain it we must touch our deeper spiritual selves and begin to see the fire. Our responses to this partnership cannot be solely cognitive. Don't mistake my points and consider that Abraham and Moses thought themselves merely as PR businessmen. Their responses were genuinely emotional. They felt for God and for those people who might not know the love of God if these events took place. Unless our partnership is built on genuine love and the desire to search for our own unique godliness within, we will never make the difference we are capable of; we will never know and love godliness the way we could have.

An example of partnership that didn't work was when Balaam was asked by King Balaak to curse the Jews. The King was aware of Balaam's ability to connect with God and have some form of conversation with Him. King Balaak feared the Jews and knew that merely fighting against them was no answer after the decimation of the Egyptians at the hands of the "Jewish God." This king wanted to create a level playing field so he asked Balaam to curse the Jewish people and perhaps that would cause the Jews to fall out of favor with their God. Balaam tried but to no avail. When he tried to curse the Jews even after knowing that God was unhappy with his request, God forced a blessing to emanate from his mouth. Balaam's suggestion wasn't based

Finding Your Soul 75

on love or a desire to help others become close to their unique relationship with God. It was a selfish desire to hurt the Jews. Balaam was a jealous man who hated the Jews because he felt that prophets like Moses outshined him. They did of course but only because he was too busy worrying about what he could get from God instead of what he could give. Judaic commentaries express Balaam's exasperated state due to feeling that he could not affect God's will. At one point, the commentaries say, Balaam asked to even bless the Jews when God refused to allow him to curse them. God says no again because Balaam's desire to bless the Jews was nothing more than a selfish ploy to feel important to God, that he can change God's will somehow, instead of a genuine, emotionally charged, loving response to God.

Now it's Your Turn

So what does this mean to you and me? It means the fire is always within us and we can see it and make it grow. It means that each of us has untold power to change the course of history, for our family, community and the world at large. It means that the only judgment to be placed upon us is a personal one that determines the energy we put forth toward our unique partnership with godliness. It means that each of us may begin to see the world in a way we've never quite seen it before.

For example, when a friend is ill what can you do about it? Naturally you can give to that friend, feel your friend's pain and work to connect with your friend. You can also pray to God for her. But what will you say to God? "Please let her live? She's a good person?" If you are genuinely in love with God then you'd want to consider God's world. Obviously, there's no question as to whether or not there is a *justification* for your friend to be ill or even pass away. But as a partner with God, He wants to hear how you think He is affecting others and yourself. You can say that this friend has children or grandchildren who depend on her and that you fear how their lives will turn out without your friend's ongoing love and nurturing. You can say that you personally depend on this person for strength and your struggle without her might seem unbearable. Create a plea that has some meat in it, something real from a real unique spirit like yourself.

Talk to God as the fiery person you can be, full of emotions, love and passion, desiring to get closer and closer to your internal soul and the godliness within. Begin seeing the world as your own, a place for which you are responsible. How will you make your mark? What is standing in your way? I don't have the answer for you but I know that what moves you will lead you to discovering your purpose and help you find your specific path.

There's a story of a rabbi who lived in a place that was considered rather ungodly. He was once asked how he was able to personally fight his desires to partake in ungodly behaviors that seemed quite normal in his community. He answered that he his haughtiness is was kept him from sin. The group he spoke to raised their eyebrows awaiting a more elaborate explanation. He indulged them and continued, "Whenever I had the desire to do something that would diminish my spirituality I used my haughtiness to remind myself, 'I am a partner with God. I can't partake in this lowly form of behavior. I'm much too special for that. I have a public image as this special partner.'" Being a partner causes certain serious demands on us but ones that lead us to more passionate and meaningful living.

So it's not our burden to figure out the entire world and what everyone else needs to do. It's our job to focus on our uniqueness, comfortable with the knowledge that God's part in this partnership is to lead us where He needs us once we open up our hearts and spirits and start walking toward the fire. Who knows what lies ahead? We only need to know we'll be there in a meaningful role.

Don't think extravagance. Even the slightest action can bring such spirituality to life. Sometimes when I think of those horrifying pictures of a poor African woman watching her starving child cry with no tears, my own heart sinks and I cry. Such sights make me wonder what is that woman's role, what unique chance has she been given? But couldn't it be that if for even one moment that woman can mother her child, hug him another time, kiss him gently on his forehead while she's so exhausted and pained that she can barely stand, couldn't it be that there is her spirituality? In that one action is her gift to life. There she has added love to this world in an immeasurable way. That mother doesn't have to be a heroine to the world, just a heroine to her child. She's a partner in this ever developing world that yearns for love in the most unlikely places.

Slow Down, You Move Too Fast, You've Got to Make the Moment Last

Miracles are abound, woven into the fabric of our lives. Your life will change immediately once you can simply drink this in. We have an unfortunate way of taking things for granted. Beautiful things happen around us. Some take it in and grow internally spiritual from it-they see the fire-and others ignore it or dismiss it. Some consistently hold the hand of their child and feel a link to infinity, others feel tired from their day and consistently want their kid to leave them alone so that they can watch television and veg out. Some are passionately invigorated by the taste of flavorful food and others consume with little focus on taste but merely want to be full so that they can move on to the next part of their day.

Few people are literally in the moment, seeing it as a small end in itself rather than a means to an end. A car ride doesn't have to be about getting you from here to there. Instead it can be about learning from the conversation you are having with your partner/child/parent in the car, the beautiful mountains you've seen a thousand times on the same road but seem ever-changing, the gentle whispers of the wind as you open your window on a warm day allowing it to blow through your hair, the miraculous wetness that might be hitting your windshield on any given day.

We are so caught up in where we're going that we rarely notice where we are.

Finding miracles everywhere begins with stopping yourself regularly and taking notice. Try breathing deeply-not as some relaxation technique. Breathing is fascinating. It's involuntary and yet we can focus on it and elevate it to something spiritual. The Talmud says that the Messiah will have a keen sense of smell. In our own culture we attribute a certain other worldly skill to our breathing. That's why you can "smell a rat," even though you might not be able to know he's a rat by seeing or hearing him. There is something quite different about our breathing and it's one you can begin to focus on in order to allow more spirituality into your life.

Breathe into your soul, deeply inhaling the meaning of life at that moment. Allow yourself to feel secure in knowing that your world is an elaborate one with surprises that can take you to new heights if you allow yourself to be aware of them. *Soul Breathing* can be the start to seeing a brighter existence within you. It helps you focus on the love when your child smiles at you. It invigorates you when you perform the simplest act of kindness because you will be connecting yourself to your spirit, that voice in you that sings during every moment of inner peace and indulgence in a spiritual world full of your very best self. When you Soul Breathe you think only of the moment and see with spiritual eyes. You sense a deeper meaning to life and notice that you are alive-really alive and living, connected to something much more than just you. Imagine during your breath that your entire life came to you for this moment, then enjoy that moment to it's fullest.

Soul Breathing is about taking a snapshot of that moment, making it last forever, an inner picture you'll build on and draw on whenever you desire.

Yesterday I saw my 13 year old daughter running at the roar of the ocean with her golden retriever, Rosie, lumbering alongside her, kicking up droplets of saltwater against the glowing horizon. Kodak moment? Absolutely. But it was so much more. I took a Soul Breath and said to myself that when I'm old and getting ready to check out and move on to my next hoorah, I'll remember that picture. I didn't need to get a camera. As a matter of fact, taking a photo would have been insulting, reducing it to a mere one dimensional print. For me, seeing my daughter's innocence and joy was beyond comprehension, a link to my inner spirit-something no picture could capture, except the one in my mind, heart and soul. I can't describe what I felt and neither can you when you have those moments of overwhelming love for another. Its your own little unique miracle and aren't you lucky to have them. I can download that picture at any moment for my spiritual pleasure *Better yet, I can allow it to have affected me in a way that makes every moment I experience after it a little more meaningful. I can draw strength later tonight from knowing what is the real definition of pleasure. I can use that picture to help me focus my energy to spiritual goals tomorrow. I can use my Soul Breathe as much as I want in any way I want.*

As I travel through life, I try taking snapshots of godliness when I'm with my family, friends, even alone with my pets. There is no end because godliness is infinite and when we create our partnership with God, we are immortal. Regularly breathing through your soul adds immeasurable happiness and depth to your life. It will help you redefine who you are and your purpose.

Developing Your Eternal Self

As a psychotherapist, I am often involved in dealing with the concept of low self-esteem. Among other things, it's believed to be at the root of divorce, abuse, murder, infidelity, suicide and every form of self-sabotage. All pain seems to reflect on how poorly the individual feels about him or herself deep down. No one feels like he deserves it all and the ones that do are called arrogant. Does it make sense that everyone seems to suffer from low self-value? Of course it does. Because without a sense of your spiritual self I hope you don't mind my saying, you are rather pathetic. I mean look at ya. How beautiful-brilliant-successful can you really be? No matter what you have, you know someone else has more of it. And no one has it all. You're so far from perfect it's hard to know where to look sometimes. And to top it off, please, you're getting wrinkles, weaker and ready for the grave with every moment. Little pockets of fat are forming, you didn't even know ear lobes could droop… I understand why your self-esteem is limited. We can exercise, make loads of money, have fame yet still suffer within when we look in the mirror.

But godliness offers you a different perspective. Imagine what it feels like to be immortal and what's more you have a chance to change this world forever. This is the special relationship you've been given by housing your inner spirit. Since godliness is a part of you, you have miraculous power as long as you can tap into your relationship with Him. It is that spirit in you that offers you the endless pool of love and life. You can find it, feel it and join it. Your self-value is tied up in your godly ability to affect life like no other. Without it you are mere aging flesh and bones. With it, you are powerful and beautiful. Now you're talking good, healthy self-esteem. But as with all meaningful relationships, it takes constant nurturing and focus.

So you, like everyone, wants to know exactly, "How do I develop this 'thing' that lives

Developing Your Eternal Self

inside me? Can you draw me a map, offer some quick daily exercises, place some ideas on audio tape so I can listen to it while I rush through life from here to there. I need answers, darn it, and I have little time to find them and put it all into practice." Yes, this is our world of today. The new and improved answer to "How are you?" is "BUSY!" If you're not busy you're nobody. Being busy can serve your spirit but only if you're busy with the right things, the infinite eternal things... What do you think they are?

◆*Exercise* ◆

List five personally infinite, spiritual, deeply meaningful, eternal things in your world that come to mind off the top of your head-don't think too much about it, just what strikes you immediately.

Okay, was your car on the list? Job, money, jewels... It's not there. It's not on anyone's quick list. I'm not saying these things aren't eternal. In fact they have an ability to be so but only because of what we bring to them. Hopefully, your list was full of love, connections to family and friends, perhaps prayer, charitable gifts, kindness, involvement with nature… Without knowing you I've guessed that your list was similar to everyone else's because all of us have a godliness within and when we allow ourselves to focus on our internal spirit, great things and thoughts come naturally-which is why the first part of finding and strengthening your spiritual self is to find your spiritual focus again and more often. Unfortunately, focusing on the spiritual pieces of life doesn't seem to be a large focus of our "BUSY" world. That world wants you to put your spirituality on hold, until you have all your ducks in a row-focus on your job, paying taxes, buy that home, get a cool car, build some debt while indulging yourself and start a family.

It's amazing how the world has been successful in turning obvious spiritual, eternal experiences into business as usual. Educating children isn't about the love between a parent and child who enjoy time together reading and learning about the world. It's about what the best video or computer game can teach. Being a Mom and Dad has lost its allure. We're made to believe that parenthood doesn't really seem so necessary because there are so many others who can teach and care for your child. Apparently you're much more uniquely needed at work. People stare openmouthed at my wife when she tells them she cares for her children as a response to the question, "What do you do?" She's brilliant, articulate and one of the smartest all around people I've ever met. People are aghast that she takes all of that genius and uses it to be a Mom. She's actually been asked, "How can you stand to be home baking cookies?"

It happens to be that my wife homeschools four of our children so she is using her well connected brain to develop curriculum for them. But this isn't her greatest asset. Her finest moments are when she loves learning with her children, teaches them genuine kindness and love for others, really hears their issues as my children literally breathe a sigh of relief when they feel she understands them. The eternal connections she makes with her children everyday is quite unique and something no one else could begin to do on the level that she does. Could she also have written a best-selling novel if she wasn't home with her children being a Mom? Absolutely. She's a gifted author and in time I believe you'll know her name rather well (if it works in God's grand scheme of things, of course). But for now, she's just so brilliant that she can see the miracles in the loving connections to those she loves and she revels in it- more than any other career success. Thank God I found her. Of course we found each other quite by chance which translates to peculiar unexplainable events which translates to godliness-that brought us together.

We've lost some of our finest moments and relegated them to others. Careers can be full of spiritual moments, helping others, making lifelong friendships. But too often, it's all been reduced to a paycheck. I don't know when we stopped searching for meaning in our daily lives but this waiting for the search to start on the weekend or after retirement or when midlife is about to drive us insane has got to stop. A woman once spoke to me for an hour about how involved she was with her pregnancy and delivery, searching to make it the most positive experience possible. But everything she worked on had to do with the health of her baby. Extremely admirable but when I asked her what it was like to have a living child that you created inside of you, she said, "oh it was fabulous, every time the baby moved inside of me, I knew it was alive and well."

"No, I mean, how'd you feel, ya know, inside your soul?"

She looked oddly at me. "Look, I've been a career person all my adult life. Getting pregnant at 37 was enough of a task. This pregnancy was never about me. It was about my baby." One of the most if not the most miraculous things we do as people, bringing life into the world, became yet another part of business as usual. It was all about the baby but the soul of the baby took a back seat to the business of babyhood. This Mom went on to give her child all of the benefits of the business of childhood-every new interactive toy for her brain, up to the minute computer technology, all the ballet and instrument lessons known to mankind. Perhaps the soul within her child would have to wait. Usually, I find most pregnant women rather attuned to their soul. They have that "glow" that people refer to. They feel the creation of life within and are more easily given to Soul Breathe and sense their eternal selves within. I try to talk with them and learn what it's like. But even pregnancy can mean little more than baby business to some proving that we can turn the most obvious spiritual experiences into less spiritual ones if we're not focused.

Music is a wonderful example of touching your soul. You can hear the depths of another's soul in music even though there are times we hear it only as a background. Sometimes, allow yourself to get into the music. Consider what must have been this creator's thoughts and feelings upon having developed it? Why does it speak to you and your eternal self?

There are meaningful moments that all of us do have the good fortune of experiencing but they just stay as isolated moments, while the business of life preoccupies our minds. People have told me things like, "Sure, who doesn't love reading bedtime stories while cuddling with their little boy for hours on a Sunday morning, but c'mon, that's not real life." "Sure, we have a great marriage on vacation and love spending time but that's not real life." "I like helping some of the newcomers at my job but who has time?" Your spirit is desperately trying to find you all of the time it can to fill you with profound seconds that can change life forever. It tugs at all of us and it's so obviously there. You don't have to search for it. You stumble upon your spirit every day. But you've been taught to focus away from it.

Why not stop right now and change your life. It isn't about tomorrow when you really have the time or money to do it right. *Life is about now because it is only the now that you can be sure of.* And even though your spirit will offer you countless opportunities to grow the next second and the next one after that, it can speak to you this moment loud and clear if you allow it.

Eternity is taking a moment, crawling inside of it and getting lost in its world as you allow it to change you-that change is with you forever and thus the moment is eternally yours. Nothing can ever take that moment away from you.

Learning to stop and crawl inside that moment is actually quite easy once you are determined to do it. It's easy because your spirit breathes within you. There is no new skill to learn, only tapping into what is already a part of you. There is nothing else as concrete as your spirituality.

Developing Your Eternal Self 95

Everything else can be lost. But your spirituality is as much you as the body that houses it except for one thing of course, your body will die and be disposed of. Your spirit will continue to flourish as long as you desire.

So draw your own map. What speaks to you? Kissing your spouse lightly on the lips, bear hugging your brother, bringing tea to your sick parent, lying quietly stroking your toddlers face as he gently floats into sleep, an opera in a language you can't translate but speaks clearly to you, a piece of music that reminds of you of your childhood or a loved deceased relative, slow car rides in the country, creating a garden, developing a program at work that helps others... There is no end to the list because there's no end to You or the experiences that you can turn into eternal, spiritual ones.

There is a Talmudic discussion about what happens to people when they pass away. One rabbi declares that God will hold each of us accountable to His questions of, "Did you see my beautiful mountains? Did you taste of my delicious fruits?" If we had not partaken, He will respond with, "Why do you think I placed them there but for you to enjoy and love Me through them?" Godliness is about an unadulterated joy of existence that exceeds simple physical pleasures of life. It adds a dimension of passion that comes only through a deep connection with the immortality of life. We are expected to love and get the most out of life. But every experience and the pleasure we can receive from it is completely tied to how deeply we feel it in our souls. Carpe Diem takes on new meaning when you feel life through your living spirit.

Running From Yourself

Of course, there are many people who complain about how busy they are and yet do little to change their lives. Unfortunately, many people are running from life itself. You might have suffered as a child and are unkind to yourself today because of it, causing you to never stop and deal

Developing Your Eternal Self

with "you." As a psychotherapist, I feel some of the most wonderful things I have done has surrounded helping others feel safe enough to delve into their past and understand how their unresolved pain has caused them to diminish their lives. But Soul Breathing is the beginning of a journey for you. You may need great help from others along the way but your soul will lead the way and let you begin to see that you are a fantastic being who lives within a world of personal miracles-You Deserve It-godliness breathes inside of you-and no one or thing from your past, present or future can take that away. *You answer to a higher authority and God isn't wasting time putting His godliness into "nobody's."* Begin to trust your unique spirituality and stop running from yourself. Get any support you need and lean on your spirit for answers. If you can begin to see the fire, it'll illuminate the answers you need.

GOD IS IN YOU

So how do you see the fire? Remember my metaphor when I notice the dust particles that were floating in front of me and I didn't notice them before the sun illuminated them? What else is right in front of me that I don't see? It's not hard to imagine that there is an entire world, a spiritual one that you have yet to discover, to have some light illuminate it for you. It might sound so beyond your normal existence or you might believe it but not know how to do it. It's not as complicated as you think.

Here is simply our greatest and only asset. Humans are created when God breathes life into the nostrils of Adam. This short sentence marks the beginning and never ending experience of humankind. Simply put, God has placed a part of Himself into each of us. Mind boggling? It would seem so. Even as I write it I know it can sound simply bizarre. But this is the crux of what I have to share. Everyone is looking outside to find spirituality. People are looking to the heavens, traveling the world to see others who will help them find meaning. There are some who meditate to find inner peace and balance but are not looking to connect with their spirit.

Your spirit is that part of God inside of you.

I don't know how He did it. But He combined His self with another item, your physical self and actually gave you some control over a piece of Him. The closest example I could muster would be to think of a parent and child. Our parents live and breathe inside of us. Every fiber and atom in us is imprinted with their genetic code. Then every part of our behavior is somehow wrapped up in how they showed us the world and helped us form our self-opinion. God has done even more. The life we have is due to His real, consistent, breathing presence within us.

Look, don't take my word for it. Your soul comes straight from God. It is your eternal source of true life and it's not hard to connect to. You don't have to look far to find spirituality. You don't need to leave your seat. It's in you and the first step is to find it in you and then build on it with all the wonders of the world that you'll now begin to see. Take the time to nurture it and it will give you immediate feelings of peace, this connected feeling I refer to. Stare at the rain and think of it with new perspective while you Soul Breathe. *Take anything that's already meaningful in your life and have it work for you, for your soul. Ponder it and force it to give to your immortal self.*

As we discussed, consider your love for others, for example, and notice that it doesn't make sense. It's not real, you can't touch it, sell it or change it but you'd give up your life for those for whom you feel it. There's much more to talk about regarding love but stop right now. Take a deep breath while saying out loud to yourself *"I am eternal. I am a soul. I will find more and more of my soul. I will see with new eyes and listen for the deeper sounds of spirituality, smell the distinct aromas that feed my immortal self, touch with soulful warmth and softness."* Am I sounding like that old skit on Saturday Night Live when Howard Smalley looks in the mirror and says, "Gosh, darn, people like me..." I'm not a believer in building yourself with empty personal gratuitous statements. I'm very, very real, I assure you. I'm not a person whose talking to himself about scriptures on the street. I'm not into the idea of looking into my mirror while reciting affirming statements. I'm not a vegetarian and I don't like oat bran (although there's nothing wrong with special diets). I live in the same physical world you do and enjoy many of the same things. I just enjoy them much more than most others.

It's a simple but powerful beginning because nothing can ever be the same once your vision sees constant miracles. It's quite overwhelming as a matter of fact. But don't let that stop you from seeing it. Don't let the intensity of it cause you to shy away. You don't have to lead some weird life where every moment you talk of God and can't work because you're too busy conversing with the rain. But changing your outlook to see that the world is full of miracles is crucial to living in a spirited world. After you've seen a little more of the fire, you'll allow yourself to go beyond the natural miracles of your day.

Consider "coincidence." Everyone has had wonderful, peculiar things happen to them. Again, it would be impossible for me to list the ones that have happened to me or to others I know. They're too numerous and limited by my own perspective. But think back to the moments in your life that you did x instead of y for no particular reason and because of it you met a lifelong friend, your spouse, your business partner. Consider the time when your plans changed suddenly causing you to end up with your child at a moment when your child really needed you. It's always happening-the question is whether or not you're noticing it. You might diminish its impact by calling it "being in the right place at the right time" or seeing it as your own sound decision making skills. But we know that all of the knowledge in the world doesn't equal success, not financially or socially. You know people smarter and better equipped than you who have failed in different areas of life and it may seem hard to believe. Yet, it's possible that they have only failed in their immediate goal, take a failed business venture, for example. From that "failure" may come the greatest gift of lessons or introductions to new worlds that may never have occurred without this seemingly awful lesson of today. Try it.

◆*Exercise* ◆

Write down ten of the most wonderful things that have happened to you in your lifetime.

Now consider the immediate events that lead to these moments. Did it go exactly as you planned? If your intention was to date and find a spouse, did you find him or her exactly as you expected? If you planned to become financially successful, did it happen as you always assumed it would? Please write me if everything in your life has followed exactly as planned, Ripley's Believe It or Not is waiting. As you review your list how many of these wonderful things have gone exactly as planned? Have you found even one that really happened exactly as planned?

Again, you could say, all of them are merely a bunch of coincidences. But as you say that you are diminishing your ability to experience a lifetime of incredible joy and meaning and the ability to become even more creative and successful in your life's goals. Join me in this quest to see and feel more than ever before and simply trust yourself. If you feel the joy of new perspective, why fight it? Enjoy it and trust your inner self and spirit. It's often much more trustworthy than logical reasoning alone.

I must interrupt. Somehow, everything happens for a reason and this must be happening now at this point in my writing for a reason as well.

Developing Your Eternal Self

As I'm typing away on my laptop now on a man made miracle referred to as a plane, I have just witnessed a rocket being blown off at NASA. The pillared trail of white smoke billowing through the sky past me is invigorating. It is powerful, stunning and oddly small as it is still swallowed up in the vastness of a large sky around me. The rocket slips out of my physical sight but stays in my internal/eternal sight forever. Imagine that trip into space. I'm there in my spirit dreaming of the vastness of life and our universe.

The world has no limit, no end. God has no limit, no end. You have no limit, no end.

What's in a Name? Your Unique Connection to God

There is one of the most telling conversations when Moses first talks to God about his new direction to free the Jews from slavery. Moses asks what he should say when the Jews ask him the name of this God. God answers, "I am what

I am." This scene is quite curious. First of all, Moses was going to tell the Jews that the "God of your forefathers" sent me. That should be satisfying as a name. Secondly, these people are starving, abused slaves. Frankly, who cares exactly what God's name is. Let's just get out of here. And the most obvious question, what kind of answer is "I am what I am." This is going to pacify their request to know this God's name?

But the Jews were right to inquire of God's name. They were going to be told that this was the God of their forefathers but they needed to know what was going to be their own personal relationship with this God. What was going to be his "name?" Was he going to be a God full of kindness, rebuke, justice, love? The request to know His name was a request to know what was going to be His definition, His relationship to His new nation.

To this question, God gives them (and us) the most powerful message of spirituality. In fact, He does not say I am what I am. It's an unfortunate translation of the Hebrew that really says, "I will be what I will be." God tells His new nation in essence that "I will be many things to many different people." Humankind is expected to receive many different parts of God. To one person, God will offer structure, to another-love, to another-justice. Every person will have the obligation and pleasure of developing his or her own relationship with God so that He will BE many different things to everyone. He will even be many different things to the same person. Sometimes you can relate to God as your Dad or Mom and other times He'll be your brother. It's up to you. He's prepared to be whatever you want Him to be.

This idea continues with the way God is referred to in the Hebrew language. There are many names for God. However, curiously, there is one term used to refer to God far more than any other in the Jewish world. It's not "Master of the World," "Great One," "Holy One," "Mighty One." The most common conversational term for God in Hebrew is

"Hashem." This has always been significant for me because Hashem means simply "The Name." Quite a peculiar choice because I think when you refer to God you should be saying something a little more profound than "the Name." Yet this was God's message to us. God is simply that, a Name. Which Name? Well, that is for you to discover and the Name you discover and choose to love may have little to do with the Name I connect to. Your Name may help you through struggle while offering you strength whereas my Name may force me to seek opportunities to love others and myself. Your Name may help you recover from a horrible past whereas and my Name may help me resolve pain in the future. Your Name may focus on learning- mine on giving. And neither of our Names ever remain constant. Ever changing, we build on what we know and what our identity has offered us thus far.

So what will be your Name? One was chosen for you by others. And it's rather important, you are identified by it and you don't like anyone making fun of it. But the one you will always be known for here and for eternity will be the one *you* choose, the relationship to your soul, the blank Name given to you within. It is a gift for you to mold and nurture. You will define it as it will define you. The more you look to grow and practice goodness for yourself and others, the more of a Name you'll have. But *you* will define your personal growth and goodness. All of us have a Name. Inside we know right from wrong, good from evil. We feel it, it's just there-it's been there since we were little. That voice of truth that breathes inside a little child is another proof that a Name lives within us developing a spiritual path far before we can cognitively reason. If you live your day knowing you are developing this Name, the miracles of life will surround you, your Name will grow and the Name will guide you and shine within you.

This Name wants a unique relationship with you and has given you His very own soul straight from Him. This Name doesn't wish you to duplicate your spirit. It's quite impossible because He's given you a unique connection/Name to Him. You may never discover this Name which would be a great tragedy, not only for you as an individual but for the world and its history. Imagine the world's loss had Abraham not chosen to challenge his teachers, had Mozart never been given an instrument as a young boy, if Van Gogh saw himself as nothing more than a madman or Shakespeare never believed in himself enough to write. *Everyone's talents are show stopping in the scheme of the history of the world. But only a few will find them. Be one of those. Make the Name your own. Be determined to grow from everything, every experience and every moment. Relate in your own way to the Name and feel how your Name can be eternally growing.*

God God God

As I speak of this uniqueness I can't help but worry that again just the mention of God makes

Developing Your Eternal Self

some people nervous. The term might conjure up memories of lecturing, being judged or a picture of fundamentalism. But I am discussing quite the opposite. Stop allowing other images of God to distance you from your unique connection. Simply put, don't let others spoil it for you. George Carlin has a bit about people who make him nervous, one of them being anyone who mentions God constantly in a sentence. I know that when God is mentioned, everyone's thoughts begin to race. God means so many things to you and unfortunately, most of what He means has probably less to do with you and more to do with what you've been "taught." Some of it may be positive and some of it negative. As a rabbi and observant Jew, I of course believe in my personal version of "organized religion." But I don't ascribe to my way of life merely because I've been taught to.

I believe what I believe and do as a I do because of the self-thought, feeling and reflection I've done in my life, of course with the help of so many, some who I sought out and some (like my parents) who were given to me. And much of it had nothing to do with specific conversations about God and religion. No, I've sought and have found spiritual growth from the one armed man who asks me for a meal at least once a week at Lincoln Road to the headmaster of my rabbinic school who taught me to question and develop answers for myself with the help of lifetimes of others who thought and discovered before me. I don't ask you to follow or do any one thing but to consider your own Name. Forget the negatives of the term "God" and what you've heard and been made to believe. Begin your own personal journey and it starts with your Name. You'll decide what that Name will be. You'll decide and God's gifts in this world and communication with you will help you every step of the way.

One slight failing of religion has been to, at times, place such an emphasis on a spiritual place- the synagogue, temple, church… and their leaders-

Developing Your Eternal Self

as if these are the exclusive bastions of faith and godliness. My relationship to religion is not only to infuse me with a greater focus of spirituality when I'm in my synagogue but to bring that focus to every part of my life. I truly believe there is as much spirituality in my home as in my synagogue or any place in the world. At the same time, I do feel however that I can relate to my spiritual self with greater ease in my synagogue than my home. I believe when I'm surrounded by other spiritual people coming together to pray or be involved in spiritual acts it offers me a strength and insight I can't have while I'm alone. So don't get me wrong. I'm a big believer in the spirituality that is offered at religious institutions. But I also believe that these institutions have a way of reducing the individual's power of feeling spiritual. Too many religious leaders may send the message that godliness seems to stay at the institution instead of traveling with the individual into every part of life. I can't envision God placing more of His presence in one building than another. God's presence is everywhere. Where and how you and I can best relate to it is something religion is trying to help us with.

Supporting this concept that spirituality is dripping in your home as in mine and any spiritual leader's is the story of Jacob and his son, Joseph, just before Jacob's death. The Torah tells us that Joseph bowed to the head of Jacob's bed. Jewish commentary explains the reason for this was because the spirit of God rests on the heads of those who are deathly ill. Again, I don't picture some angelic swoosh of godliness moving in quickly toward an ill person's head much the way I see those swirling hurricanes coming at us on the radar screen. Rather, I imagine that a person who is quite ill has a greater sense of spirituality, can see the fire clearer and can accept and bring out the treasure trove of godliness that fills every part of our world. When we are sick and weak, we look to our immortal selves and begin to see that our physical bodies are mere packaging for something within that is far superior. Joseph can sense the holiness in the room and bows to its awesome place that it has taken in his world. We don't have to be sick to look within and find our spiritual selves. The miracles are always there and begging us to take notice.

Religions offer us a means to an end, commandments meant to help us see the fire. Curiously, there are those who can follow commands and never see the fire, never genuinely fall in love with God. They can be religiously observant and yet largely devoid of spirituality. Sometimes people can get caught up in the observance and the *energy* to do them while losing the *synergy* between observance and spirituality. I follow the Jewish religion and believe strongly in its principles and laws. But I know that each one of them is there to develop within me the love for godliness. I know that my commitment to keeping one law will have a completely different flavor than that of someone else's commitment to the same law. And that is why religion is still extremely gray even though it is too often seen as black and white. God left us plenty of flexibility because He gave us each a piece of Him, our own soul. If God wanted to make us into his little robots, He would have written the 50 books of Moses instead of the five books. He would have written every detail of what we should do from the second we awaken to the second we sleep for every year we live. But he didn't because He wants an ever developing relationship and we need the flexibility to find our own personal way to love Him.

This is the strength of Your Name, the internal spirit you have. You can shape it to bring as much spirituality as you desire in your life. You don't have to travel to find it. It's inside of you and godliness is everywhere waiting to have someone like you find it.

When a so called "religious leader" begins to dictate and espouse a single way to reach godliness that offers little or no flexibility, fundamentalism is created. And this is what makes so many of us (myself very much included) anxious. Consider how many people have been killed and continue to be murdered in the name of religious leaders who are so called "speaking for God." Unfortunately, even the moderate religious leaders among us often don't realize that God wants every one of us to have a personal, loving relationship with Him. The desire to "teach" should be only to suggest paths by which each individual can declare him or herself a partner with God.

At the same time, it isn't fair to allow any form of fundamentalism to cause the rest of us to abhor the discussion of God, wincing as if someone had made a statement involving the words "colon and kidney" during dinner. The publishing world has at times been fearful of anything to do with God in their titles. They properly worry that readers will pass these books on the shelves as quickly as they pass a screaming preacher or rabbi discussing sin and repentance. Even though 85% of Americans claim to believe in God it doesn't seem that publishers eagerly seek to produce books to speak to this interest. Or perhaps God books always seem to be telling people what to do instead of helping readers find greater spirituality from within. Either way, for our purposes godliness is about forming a very personal partnership. No one should be allowed to diminish this greatness you have within you. Take a fresh approach to godliness by starting to find it within leaving no one else's expectations to guide you otherwise.

◆*Exercise* ◆

Spiritual Goals

I've heard of writing down your life goals, family goals, business goals, marital goals… the most important one, however, is your spiritual goal.

What is Your Name? What do you want your spirit to look like, feel like, be known as eternally? Write a one sentence answer. It'll change but start considering it right now.

Developing Your Eternal Self

Next, underneath your one sentence, list what you can begin to do to focus on your spirit, polish your internal godliness. Be as detailed as you can. Think about those moments you feel something "other"-different that just feeling good-the moments you feel all warm inside, at peace, valuable to yourself and others.

Once you focus on your spirit you'll find "surprises" that will help you along the way. Your Name will guide you and the "coincidences" of your day will draw you closer and closer to your spirit.

Recently after returning from a trip to the British Museum, I told a friend how I touched a sarcophagus that was over three thousand years old. I was deeply moved by that "first" experience. "There aren't too many opportunities to touch anything three thousand years old," I remarked proudly. My friend laughed and said, "Yeah, except the dirt under you every second of the day." I must admit I felt foolish. But what a door that opened for me. I can connect to an eternity of years by touching the ground. Is it odd for me to stop and find plush green grass to touch with my hands or bare feet? Is there a better feeling for our feet than walking of fresh supple grass? Often, the best spiritual experiences are the best physical ones as well. Is it odd for me to simply pick up some dry dirt or sand and focus on it as it lightly dribbles through my fist as I try to crawl into a moment-to take a deep breath and capture it? My mind wanders and thinks of others who walked on this dirt, the crust of our existence. The beginning of humankind created miraculously from ends of the earth, we're told in the Torah, and to where our finite bodies will one day return melding together for a peaceful, eternal union. In my hands I have found life in that simple dirt that just yesterday was insignificant to me.

Recently, I had lunch with a friend of mine who is a rabbi of a large, prominent synagogue. In the midst of our conversation he asked me, "Be real

Developing Your Eternal Self 121

with yourself. If there was no God, would you act any differently?" I was perplexed. I responded with a resounding yes still unsure of what his question could possibly mean. Then he told me his own answer, "No." He explained that he acts out of kindness for others and he'd do that no matter what. I understood him. My friend saw spirituality as a kind of humanism; a kindness and love for others and the world. But how was that "spirituality" as opposed to benign acts of kindness? I think love does come from a "spirit," God's very hand. See, he and I might be doing similar actions at the start. But when he does something kind for another, for example, he might not feel any more connected to His inner Name. He must feel good but he may stop it from reaching his soul, from changing his eternal light within. He probably feels good because it is touching his deeper spirit but may be stopping it from developing his intense relationship with godliness. *When I help another, I am often overcome with joy, not because I only helped someone, but because I'm involved in this grand picture of connecting to another part of my Name, the godliness in me. I feel this internal tug that tells me I'm so alive-yes, I'm godly at that moment. Maybe my entire life continues because of that moment. Who knows what I've done and how I've affected life and history? I smile at the miracles of God, letting me be involved with another part of Him because the person I just helped is yet another unique spirit, piece of God.*

There's a story of a student that once approached his Chasidic teacher and asked, "Teacher, how are you and I so different? We follow the same laws. For example, when I'm about to eat an apple, I say the bracha (Jewish blessing said over food) and when you eat an apple, you make the same exact blessing."

The teacher answered, "The difference is that you make the blessing so that you can eat the apple. I, on the other hand, eat the apple so I can make the blessing."

Spiritual people are looking for opportunities to connect to their Eternal Names. They're not waiting for a poor person to come along so they can give some charity. They're forever searching out experiences that will feed their soul. They're searching to bring more love into their lives and feel at one with their internal godliness. What can you do today to search for a moment of godliness?

Abraham-Searching for Kindness was His Name

The Torah tells the story of Abraham sitting outside of his house on the third day after his circumcision. He was the first man to be circumcised. At the ripe age of 99 years old, the circumcision showed his dedication to God and the desire to "perfect" himself. Abraham had a fantastic partnership with God, one in which God clearly cared for him directly like a parent. On this particular day, God tried to save Abraham the effort he'd put forth in caring for guests. Abraham took special pleasure in caring for others and his home was known as an open to the public kind of place. To make his home especially inviting, he built a door on every side of his home so that people could enter from any direction. He and his righteous wife Sarah, regularly cooked and served tourists and locals.

God caused the sun to shine intensely on that day, a day when Abraham was particularly weak from his surgery, in order to save Abraham the effort to serve visitors. God knew that the only way to get Abraham to take a break would be to cause the day to be so hot that people would stay indoors. Now, if it were you or me, we'd be relieved. No visitors, terrible day, crawl into bed with a good DVD. But Abraham didn't take this brutally hot day as a sign that he could rest. He still sat outside his home absolutely desperate to find someone to welcome into his home. He was terribly sad that no one was walking the streets that day. God felt so bad for him that He ended up sending a few angels to satisfy Abraham's desire to welcome guests.

The reason Abraham was the father of Judaism and respected by all religions is because he understood spirituality. He didn't welcome guests because it was the "right thing to do" or "it was a commandment." He genuinely loved God and the eternal, unique spirit he was given. He saw the "fire" all of the time and it gave him a euphoric feeling. His ability to connect with other souls and unique spirits was akin to eating and drinking for him. He couldn't be happy unless his soul was in full swing, experiencing meaningful moments which for him came largely at the hand of his kindness to others. He searched for meaningful moments and would not rest until he found them.

When searching for spirituality feels like a chore, we're in the wrong ballpark. Of course there are times when sacrificing or doing an action that seems arduous at the moment might not seem like fun and thus feel chore-like, but we should experience a "wow" feeling from completing our task if we allow ourselves to do so. It's a natural feeling in our souls. Too often we tend to let it pass and rarely focus on it. We want to give ourselves a few moments to think about what just happened and how we can connect to our inner name because of this moment. All you need to do is direct yourself a little and your soul will take over and do the rest. *Start seeing opportunities in your life to become more spiritual*-hug your child, touch a tree and smell a flower, greet a stranger, kiss your lover, call that friend in the hospital or who you know is a little down, pray, ponder deeply within yourself, go to that lecture about God, start reading that book about godliness… And don't let the good feeling pass without focus. *Close your eyes and just feel great that you've loved someone or helped someone-feel more alive-begin to feel the fire before moving on. Take that fantastic soul you were given and make it a partner with God.*

Abraham shouts to us all to be ourselves. For example, Abraham who has impacted many religions, was not your typical proselytizing fellow. Perhaps you think the great Abraham walked the streets like the town crier, carried a hand bell, sung God's praises, told people to believe, showed them how to pray, made them feel guilty for not being involved in godly pursuits. If you met Abraham for the first time, do you know what he'd do? Offer you dinner. He'd invite you into his home and he and his wife, Sarah, would cook and serve you a wonderful meal. He'd probably talk about random thoughts including the local sports team. And guess what? You would have left a different person. Not because Abraham tried to convince you to be more spiritual. But because you would have felt this really special aura around Abraham. You would have sensed that he was godly even though your entire conversation might have never turned to the subject of God. You would have started to think what was different about him and how can you get in on his peacefulness. You'd return tomorrow figuring at the very least you'll get one of the best cooked meals in town. And before you knew it, you'd be asking Abraham how you can be more godly and how you could find *your* inner Name.

Abraham found his godliness through kindness and it was his kindness that brought others to believe in their own godliness. *Kindness lies at the very heart of our soul and it is the first and foremost lesson to seeing the fire. After all, none of us would be here if not for the kindness of others.* God was kind enough to give us life and our parents or guardians were kind enough to protect and nurture that life. There is a reason we come into this world as needy infants who would die within hours if not for the kindness of others. God sets the stage for us. *It is out of kindness that we are created and able to live. Kindness is not just something one does. Kindness is life giving. It is encoded in our spiritual DNA. Giving and finding kindness will always rejuvenate and develop our Name.* That is why Abraham seeks to offer kindness. He knows it is the one genuine pursuit that every organism requires. It must be godly. He discovers and creates a lifestyle in which kindness is his primary source of spirituality.

Rebecca, Navigating Life Through Kindness

This same character is then sought out by his servant, Eliezer, when he is sent to find a bride for Abraham's son, Isaac. As Eliezer traveled to find an appropriate match he makes a deal with God. As Eliezer approaches the town's community well, he creates this sign for God to indicate that Isaac's soulmate is at hand. If a girl offers Eliezer water when he stops at the community well and she then offers to also get his camels water; that will be the bride for Isaac. As he finishes talking to God, indeed, Rebecca approaches and offers Eliezer *and* his camels water, even though she is young (some say three years old-unbelievable? Shouldn't be when you consider that Mozart was writing music at five) and it'll take her many trips to quench the thirst of many camels.

Eliezer was a vibrant, able bodied man. He had recently helped Abraham defeat four kings in a brutal war and he now traveled with quite an entourage to find a bride for his master's son. He didn't need help getting water from a well or getting water for his camels. If a young man were to approach me in a building and ask me where the water fountain was, I wouldn't respond with, "Sit right there and I'll get you some water and I'll get some more water for your friends too." I would simply tell that young man where the fountain was and think nothing more of it. Eliezer is a strong individual who doesn't need the help of little girl. In fact, I'd question if it's even considered "kindness" to bring him water when it's nothing for him to do it himself. Is it a kindness to give a millionaire a dollar? If Eliezer wants to see if Rebecca is kind then create a test surrounding her running to help an old lady, calm a stranger's baby or lend an item to someone in real need.

Yet, Eliezer's test is spiritually brilliant. He's not attempting to discover if Rebecca is kind. He's determined to find someone who is always searching for spiritual connection. Rebecca is delighted to help an old lady in need. But if no old lady is to be found, she will not rest-the same way Abraham would not rest if there was no visitor to welcome. Rebecca's soul was desperate to seek out experiences that helped her define her Name. Abraham and Rebecca used kindness as a way to navigate life. Most people are kind because they feel it's ethically appropriate or they feel really warm inside helping another in need. But Abraham and Rebecca's kindness was about that and much more. They used kindness as a way to connect to other souls. They believed the world was created out of kindness and continues out of kindness and thus, they felt that the supreme method of connecting to godliness was through kindness.

That's why Rebecca sought to do for the capable Eliezer even though he could've easily cared for himself.

I'm afraid I might have told Eliezer to take a walk while pointing out the well. I would be too busy, have lots of personal excuses as to why I should move on. But Rebecca sought connection through kindness. Now that she was kind to Eliezer she'd find out who he was, where he was from and much more about his mission. She'd learn a thing or two from him and in the meantime help him connect to her brand of godliness, her unique Name. *Abraham and Rebecca are adventurers, explorers into a constantly changing and expanding world of spirituality. They eat the apple in order to be able to make the blessing. They are seekers and because of that energy, they constantly grew their Inner Name.*

Growth Through Seeing Another Perspective

That search was their own brand of connection. What are we if we can't connect to other life? Remember that dust before? The "fire?" How do we ever see what we haven't seen before? It comes through connection. As you allow yourself to feel what someone else is feeling, you place yourself in someone or something else's shoes. You grow your perspective and never again can you be just the person and spirit you were before. When you read a book or see a movie, for example, you allow the creator of that book or movie to show you a perspective you possibly have never seen before. When you consider what is must be like to be someone else, an animal, a flower, anything outside of you, your soul begins to develop and you become more sensitive to the world around you. You become connected to things outside of you and this makes you far larger than you were before.

Consider the message God gives us when He creates breathing. You can't live for more than minutes without breathing. And every single breath you take comes from the same source that everyone and everything else in the world uses. You are forcibly connected to every other part of nature whenever you breathe. You are dependant on others to be able to breathe. If someone plants fragrant trees, your breathing is richer due to it. If someone sprays the air with toxins, you suffer. You and I are not only connected to other people, but to our pets and plants, our sun and rain, every part of nature that works symbiotically to keep our atmosphere oxygenated. It can't be coincidental that one of the most commonly agreed relaxation technique is simply taking a deep breath.

Let me tell you, much of the good in our lives is a by chance kind of thing that happens through the kindness of others. I only found a top literary agent after I was on a talk show and I asked the host who didn't know me from Adam if she knew an agent. She made the call for me out of the kindness of her heart (there was absolutely nothing tangible in it for her) and connected me to a dynamite agent who enabled me to then meet wonderful people at Random House... Every part of my life was made through the kindness of others, kindness of connections. I got on the Oprah show because my wife asked half jokingly to friends we just met at dinner, "Does anyone here know Oprah?" And of course, in godly coincidental form, a gentleman said that as a matter of fact, his brother had been engaged to a producer there. Even though the engagement didn't work out, both ended up marrying others and were happy. He made the call even though he hadn't spoken to her in eight years. She was the top producer, one that my PR people at Random House couldn't get to. My personal stories of how the kindness of others have shaped my life are endless, both personally and professionally and if you think about it, so are yours.

The Battle of the Sexes

This growth through understanding different perspectives explains another phenomenon-why God created man and woman with such differences. Whenever couples argue they lose their fantastic ability to grow spiritually. God purposely made man and woman so different so that each could learn about new ways to see and experience life. There's no purpose to marrying someone that you have nothing to learn from. As we experience life together with our partner, we're to indulge in our differences. Every single difference holds a lesson about life, a new perspective that you haven't seen before. Whether or not you agree becomes irrelevant. *Life is not about winning and losing but rather taking the godliness we have been given and uniquely nurturing it.*

The next time your spouse is seeing life differently, take the time to listen to it-ask follow up questions. Don't assume you already know exactly what your spouse means. Give yourself the opportunity to grow your godliness by understanding a different perspective. In fact, originally, Adam was created with the ability to give birth to children himself without any need for anyone else. But this is exactly what disturbed God. He felt that man would lose himself in his egotistical ability to procreate and feel too godly, forgetting his attachment or need for God. So God created Eve. Now man would not be able to procreate on his own but must have a woman. How will he get a woman? Hopefully, he will woo her, be kind and warm and help her love him. No longer would he be able to have children because he wanted to but now he'd first need to relate to someone else-someone quite different than him. This would force man to nurture his spirit through growing his own perspective-simply relating to woman, a being he'd work forever to understand.

Why did God go through this game of creating Eve later? Clearly God knew man by himself wouldn't work out even before he created him. Interesting enough, when we are told in the Torah that God feels, "It is not good for man to be alone," the next sentence does not say that Eve was created. Immediately after there are a couple of sentences that describe how Adam named all of the animals. He sees that every animal has a partner, an opposite gender, except for him. Only then in the next sentence does God place Adam in a deep sleep and create Eve. It seems that it wasn't enough for God to realize that Adam needed a wife. Adam had to realize it. Only after he was saddened by seeing other animals enjoying their partners could God create Eve. Now when Eve would offer a different perspective, Adam would understand that he wanted and needed that perspective to grow. Life without her was lonely, sad and offered limited growth. *Your spouse offers you powerful growth because no one else in the world will be both so different than you and so intimate with you. You will be privy to the intimacy of deep thoughts and feelings of only one person of the opposite sex. Learn to grow spiritually from your spouse as much as you can.*

The Talmud was completed approximately 1,500 years ago. It contains volumes of intensely deep analysis of Jewish law. You'd think that the Talmud would primarily be searching to give a final answer to Judaism's most complicated legal questions. Instead, practically every page of its thousands of pages of Talmud is filled with Rabbis disagreeing with each other about different legal issues. In fact, rarely is there a time when the Talmud doesn't ask why each rabbi involved in the disagreement didn't state the same principle as the other. Rarely does the Talmud ever offer a definitive statement regarding any law. This is because the rabbis recognized that the important point was not whether or not you followed one rabbi's opinion or the other. Clearly you couldn't go wrong with either opinion. Instead the rabbis knew that the greatest growth would come from hearing many different perspectives. Right or wrong isn't the issue even in legal matters in the Talmud. Understanding and absorbing different ideas and attitudes from spiritual people is what counts. The Talmud never misses an opportunity to offer as many spiritual perspectives as possible.

Growing comes from observing. Learn to say three simple words and life will open up for you in ways you never realized it could.

"Tell Me More," will invite you into other perspectives on life that you'd never see by telling your opinions or thinking your own thoughts. Often, we're a little too busy letting people know how we think.

Our Inner Name will be defined by how we absorb the world around us, translate it and turn around and act on it. It is vital that connection, true sensitivity to life around us, take place so that we can grow. Slowing yourself down from sharing and being more willing to be shared with gives you the opportunity to see another perspective. Connecting is an act of being alive and makes you a part of the grand scheme of things.

Remember that the next time an Eliezer crosses your path and you think you're too busy to spend a moment and get to know him. Show kindness in a smile, an inquiry into the other person's life, doing something helpful for the other person in some simple way. Then give yourself the moment after to feel it-that soul feeling-the unexplainable feeling of euphoria that can overtake you if you let it. Take the soul breath and connect yourself a little deeper to every part of nature.

Part Two: Setting Up Your Day for Spirituality
Three Fathers-Three Paths-Daily Living

Along my spiritual journey I discovered a certain pattern that I thought could help anyone specifically designate spirituality as part of their daily living.

Isn't it wonderful that incredibly spiritual people can be incredibly different and nurture their spirits in incredibly different ways? This reinforces the concept that no one can offer you a prescription of how to find godliness. Each of us has to find it for ourselves much the way most crucial lessons in life are self-taught once we are steered in the right direction. But the Torah has offered us glimpses of those who took bold steps to find themselves and left an impressionable mark on this world because of it. Judaism was born when Abraham devoted himself to God. He is considered the first father of Judaism. His sons, Isaac and Jacob, become the other two fathers of Judaism, each adding

Setting Up Your Day for Spirituality

immeasurably to the definition of godliness. These three Patriarchs are prime examples of how godly people can find such different ways to nurture their spirit. These fathers offer us supreme insight into how to reach for our godliness and see our "fire." We can combine their approach to experience life daily in a satisfying spiritual way.

Jewish law teaches that Jews are to pray three times daily. The reason is that each of the Patriarchs introduced a special time for prayer during their lifetime. Abraham instituted a morning prayer, Isaac-afternoon prayer, Jacob-evening prayer. Each one had his unique connection and method of searching and finding godliness and each found a focused time of his day to clearly connect to God. For me, this has always taught me a personal lesson about a twenty-four hour period. Obviously, the method each patriarch used to find spirituality related to a certain time of day that best served his ability to grow. The day can be divided into three parts and we can focus on the character trait of each patriarch during that period of the day and have fabulous results. They knew (they could sense it as they saw their own "fire") that sewn into the fabric of these parts of the day were the ability to use different character traits as spiritual methods of connecting to life around us and our Inner Name. Simply put, you can get more power for your punch, more bang for your buck, if you focus on certain traits during certain parts of the day.

Morning

The Beginning of Everything-KINDNESS

Abraham navigated life as he connected through kindness. Being the first man to be able to convince others of monotheism, he had a unique gift of showing his spirituality through his kindness. *It would make sense to start off your day with the start of life itself. All life begins with kindness.* Every child would die if not for the sacrificing kindness of another, usually parents who must immediately cater to every need of their child. It is true of most life, animals depend on parents for varying amounts of time. Even plant life, although not everyone may see it as a kindness, depends on sun and moisture, God's kindness, to grow. Naturally, human beings and the world as a whole were developed by God out of kindness. It's hard to use our limited selves to suppose why God created us but one Talmudic sage clearly states the reason as, "God wanted to bestow his kindness on us." He's rooting for us much the way a parent hopes her child will make the right choices and be rewarded with personal happiness. Every parent brings a child into this world realizing that child might experience severe pain and tragedy. But even with this knowledge we bring kids into this world because, in part, we have a need to give, to love a part of ourselves. God in much the same way created each of us, desiring to love a part of Himself, needing to give.

Abraham begins his journey with this simple thought. He taps into the most basic of character, kindness. He feels that God has created him and sustained him out of kindness and life cannot get past day one without other things, be it parents or nature, giving to it. He decides to be a giver and use that as his MO. This decision serves him and the rest of humankind well. Since Abraham is actively in love with his Inner Name and life itself, his genuine desire to be kind is quite intoxicating to others.

Noah vs. Abraham

Keep in mind that Abraham was far from the first righteous man or person who spoke to God. Noah came on the scene ten generations earlier and he was one powerful force in the world. Let's face it, he saved humanity and the animal kingdom as we know it. But it seems that Noah had a severe limitation. He is asked to build an ark in his yard which ends up being the longest running personal project in history, 120 years. But does he need so many years to produce this ark? Obviously not. Clearly, the ark serves as a floating miracle anyway. The dimensions that the Torah offers for this ark fall extremely short of being able to physically contain pairs of every animal. If it will be a miracle to house all of these animals on this ark anyway, why ask Noah to spend 120 years building it? Once God is already making a miracle why not make a small boat that takes a month to build and magically get everyone and every animal on that boat? Clearly, God is not looking forward to destroying the world.

He'd much rather people recognize their criminal behavior toward each other and change His intention to destroy everyone. As we've explained, everyone is given the opportunity to make a difference, change the course of history, and everyone in that generation had such an ability. So God creates this situation where Noah must hammer away year after year to create this absurdly large watercraft.

What's going to happen while Noah builds? Well, if you build it, people will come. Indeed they did. People couldn't help but ask Noah why he was building the largest boat they've ever seen in his yard which by the way was not waterfront property. The Torah doesn't record what Noah's response was. What we do know is the number of people Noah was able to convince to see the "fire" and tap into their unique godliness-ZERO. That's right. In one hundred and twenty years he was not able to make a positive impression on anyone. What did Noah say when asked about his shipbuilding? Being that Noah was a straight laced man in a animalistic society full of murder and thievery, he simply may have foretold the destruction of the world. He may have had very little patience for people of such ill morality. If so, his approach would not have been one of love and kindness, not one of connection but one of harsh reproach. In essence, Noah didn't invite people in to see his essence. He expected people to simply do the right thing without giving them a method, a window into his personal godliness. The result was a failed society and God's need to have Noah help Him build a new one.

Abraham might have learned from Noah's limitations or simply sought God in his own unique way which led him to kindness. He instituted the concept of praying first thing in the morning upon starting his day and planning the rest of his day around kindness. The message for our daily plan then begins with how all life begins, because of the kindness of others. We awake in the morning through God's kindness and should begin our own day by connecting to our world through such kindness. Interesting enough, I'm afraid that when we think of kindness we tend to believe it's something we do when we have all of our ducks in a row. We give charity when we have a lot of money one day. We call a friend whose been a little down at the end of our day or at lunch when we've accomplished much of our expected work. We visit someone in the hospital at night when we have free time. Abraham has called to us to see his vision as the start of our day, not the end of it. Upon awaking we should immediately count our blessings, the kindness of others that allows us to start our day.

It's wise to remember God, our parents, the love of our spouse and children and the people who have helped us get where we are.

Try this. *Awaken each day and upon opening your eyes, simply recall one kind thing anyone has ever done for you.* Don't pop out of bed to zip along and lose yourself and your spirit in a busy world. Take a moment to Soulbreathe while recalling a loved one who has been kind to you.

You can recall a certain incident (the time my Mom went on the roller coaster with me in spite of her bad back because I was afraid to go alone or when my spouse was so reassuring when I was considering changing professions) instead of an esoteric package (Remember Mom was nice to me or how much my spouse loves me). Specific memory will speak to your spirit immediately and help you feel connected and loved right away.

Next, start your day off with giving kindness to a loved one with whom you live. Kindness can be any form of giving. It could be a good morning kiss, hug or verbal compliment. But start your day off with giving and sharing of your spirit with someone you love. If you live with many loved ones (I am blessed with a wife, kids and many pets) focus on a different loved one each day as a start and continue to add people daily until you can give to all of them every day. If you live alone (if you have a pet I don't consider that living alone- your pet would be your loved one for the purpose of this kindness) call, write or email someone within the first half hour of getting up just to say hello and inquire as to how they are. You may already do all of this. But even for those of us that do, it's often become a habit lacking focus on really trying to connect. I mean, there's a difference between the peck on the cheek and a meaningful kiss, a pat on the head of a young child and a warm hug, a silent walk with your dog and meaningful chatter with your dog while regularly saying her name in a cutesy voice non-dog owners deem as odd.

Have in mind to connect-that you want to feel a little closer to this other living thing through your kindness.

Now consider who in your life could use some kindness. Perhaps there is that friend that is ill, down, financially strapped. Take the mental thought and heartfelt feeling to consider what you can do this morning to make a difference to that person. It may only be a phone call to say hi and that you were thinking of this person. It may be a phone call to another who might be able to help your friend or loved one. Again, often we think of making the call to help someone after the "important" business or personal calls are all out of the way. And of course if we don't have time for that call by the end of our day, it'll wait until tomorrow when we've completed our tasks for that day. Instead, develop your day with kindness. The morning holds something special for us-a unique empowerment through kindness.

What is really sad is that so many of us are already doing kind things but don't even feel warm doing them. Whenever I ask a couple to create a list of things that they appreciate about their spouse, I always get a very short list. I look at them curiously, surprised at what is missing on their list.

"What about the great parent she/he is, the great wage earner he/she is?" I ask.

And it's always the same reply, "She's supposed to be a great mother, it's his job to make a living." Somehow if we effectively do what is expected of us, it carries little weight. All of us have to recognize that we could be doing a far worse job at everything we do. There are so many moments in our day that we could be a little more selfish and give less to others. The fact that you're expected to give kindness to your child or spouse doesn't diminish your kindness. We don't take the time to feel good when we've helped our children, cooked for them, worked hard for them. We should be feeling warm and fuzzy inside because we are practicing kindness with people who depend on that kindness. Live inside those kind moments and translate them for what they are: pure, unadulterated kindness.

Your entire day will change, your spirit will see glimpses of the "fire" you've never seen before if you start your day with kindness. Visit your friend in the hospital before anything else, not at the end of your day. Finally, always take time to pray. We'll discuss what that means but for now just remember that your morning prayers should surround kindness, meditating about how kindness makes the world go round and how you can be a part of developing the world with your own pure kindness.

Afternoon

Blending Spiritual and Corporeal-Real Strength

Isaac is perhaps the most mysterious figure of the patriarchs because unlike Abraham and Jacob there is very little spoken of him as a character unto his own. He is of course known for his courage in following his father's lead and allowing Abraham to almost slaughter him. Isaac, opposed to popular belief, was thirty-six years old at the time and fully capable of not going along for the ride. But the story is written in such a way that it seems much more about Abraham's test of faith and courage than Isaac's. The next most famous story of Isaac is when Jacob pretends to be his brother Esau in order to trick Isaac into giving him a more profitable blessing. Isaac is old, sight impaired and seemingly dancing on the edge of senility. Again, the focus of this story is Jacob and his ability to maneuver around the truth while still maintaining his pure state of spirituality. Isaac seems useless in this story except for the obvious fact that contained in him are blessings worth fighting and possibly lying for. These stories do tell a great deal about Isaac. But there is one and only one story that centers around Isaac as a main character and it is one few people know although it is written in the Torah as clearly as any other story.

It is a simple and short story about Isaac's desire to dig a well. He is desperate to sink wells. As a matter of fact his first objective as the star of his own show is to try and re-dig all of the wells that Abraham had completed which were promptly plugged up. Isaac clearly wants to dig wells for reasons other than to have water as it appears he digs Abraham's wells with the knowledge that he'll be leaving town because King Avimelech has kindly asked him to exit quickly. After moving, he digs another well and others argue with him and claim it's now their well. Isaac relinquishes his right to this well and even gives the well a name that alludes to that disagreement. He then digs another well which is plugged up by the Philistines and finally digs a well that is left alone. Isaac then blesses God at this well. For a story fit to be in the Torah, it seems rather innocuous.

What is the lesson about this seeming obsession about digging wells as well as everyone's obsession around Isaac to plug up the wells? Yet this sole story about Isaac gives us great insight into whom Isaac was. It isn't a story about the need for water. Isaac was extremely wealthy and maintained a huge household and cattle. Clearly there was something meaningful happening or else others wouldn't be trying to plug up the wells. No, this was a very personal mission for Isaac. It was his signature action for finding his spirituality, seeing and building his own "fire." Isaac, like his father, is searching for God and a method to show others His presence. Abraham largely used his own kindness and personality. Isaac, however, doesn't have the need to find God as Abraham did. He was given God on a silver platter and as such begins to search for ways to bring God down to earth in clear ways. He takes everything he's learned and improves on it by finding methods to enhance living with clear godly direction. He wants to offer the world undeniable signs of godliness and then move on to help others do the same.

His tool? Well, he digs wells. Isaac sees water as godly. After all, from where do we get our water? It falls from the sky. It's a hidden treasure deep in our earth. We don't create it. It is a gift from God. Isaac sees water as an undeniable proof that God gives to us (using His brand of kindness, again, tapping into what his father, Abraham, had taught him) and Isaac sees this water as a fantastic way to connect with his Inner Name. He digs wells and moves on knowing full well that when people see his testimony that God gives to us and is directly involved with our daily life, they will want to search for their own unique godliness within. It is his monument to spirituality and obviously one that others who didn't want such testimonies detested.

The Jewish religion and many others use water as a purification process. There is something extraordinary about water and being enveloped in it. Slow movements in the ocean or any body of water seems primal and speaks to our spiritual name. Isaac tapped into this strength of nature to surround his Name with godliness.

Isaac spread his wings. He was trying to find ways to help others begin their journey without needing such personal involvement like his Dad which had it's obvious drawbacks. He wanted to spread out his message using his father's lessons. But in so doing, Isaac developed a powerful, unique message himself.

He developed a character of combining our real, corporeal selves with spirituality. He wanted to show how every physical thing, every physical experience had in it a powerful, undeniable, spiritual one.

Abraham believed this as well but his route was one of patience and getting to know people, there was a softness about his approach (not to say Abraham was soft when it came to doing the right thing-He was as stand up a person as anyone could be. When he was told that his cousin Lot's shepherds were technically stealing grass by allowing their cattle to graze on other people's fields, he tells Lot in no uncertain terms to choose one direction and Abraham would be headed in the exact opposite one). Isaac had this genuine purity about him, the purity that comes with lack of spiritual struggle. It allowed him to infuse godliness into the simplest parts of life. He knew how to get the message of God across and not in a "damning you to hell" way, or an "I can debate you until you admit I'm right" way. Rather in a simple, powerful, see the undeniable interaction God has with us, kind of way. He wanted to show people everywhere that you don't have to travel to Abraham's tent to see God. You don't have to be touched by Abraham's kindness to feel God. For heaven's sake, don't you see it raining? Can't you sit by the well and recognize God's ongoing place in our lives? The ones who plug up the well do so because they don't want this God stuff to catch on. They are committed to their way of life and don't want it to be questioned about it or perhaps don't wish to confront themselves. They plug them up. But after a while they realize that it won't work. Isaac is going to keep digging wells until they stop. There is nothing they can do because his purity is such that his godliness grows every moment as he searches for godliness in water. His strength wins out. He digs and they finally let him have his living monuments to godliness.

Isaac becomes synonymous with strength. But not the muscular kind. The kind that shows unflagging devotion to a cause he believes in. The kind that takes real honest strength-showing the world and himself that our physical selves are nothing more than packaging for an immortal soul.

He could have pumped up his own ego by using his father's wealth and his ingenuity. But he didn't feel any need for that. *His strength was about recognizing truths and showing them to others without debate.* Isaac gives us a picture of great power-the power to see godliness in our physical world and the power to bring that message to the rest of the world without fear, without ever considering stopping, even if others make it difficult for you.

Isaac institutes the concept of afternoon prayer. It is his way of finding time to connect with his Inner Name and use his power to again clearly get in touch with how much godliness there is in his physical world. *Our day needs to be about power-Isaac power. The strength to devote ourselves to our beliefs and live a lifestyle that shows how godly we are.* Isaac power means finding ways of living and interacting that show we are spiritual beings. Not by telling people we're godly or warning them that the sky is falling if we don't repent, but in an Isaac fashion-unflagging devotion to the personality we've chosen that helps us see spirituality in every day events. Naturally, this is quite a unique experience. But begin to consider what do you do or say in a day that helps you and maybe others see the "fire" a little more? Perhaps it's using comforting, spiritually meaningful words with a colleague who is discussing a problem, "Things have a way for working out for the best. Think back to so many times when you probably thought what was happening wasn't so great but it turned out to be good for you. You just didn't see it that way for a while. Maybe use this time to get closer to some of those people you've been too busy to spend time with lately."

Maybe it's developing a group at work dedicated to helping others. Perhaps it's being a person of integrity and honesty in a job that doesn't often find people so true to their spiritual compass. You will make a lasting impression on others if you show the strength of being up front and absent of hidden agendas. You don't need to talk about God to be godly. You need only to allow your spiritual self to come out. That could come with a certain inner peace or willingness to be kind. Did you ever meet someone and just feel they had a special aura? You can't necessarily point to any one thing they said or did but you just feel that the way they held themselves was special. That was Isaac and that could be you.

It's easy to go to a religious institution and feel holy. But God's intention was for us to live a life out there in the real world and bring spirituality to it. Our day should be a powerful display of our faith to our godliness, our desire to be true to ourselves and constantly search for ways to see the "fire" even in the midst of seemingly non-spiritual situations. If your day is about muddling through an unimportant job, bring importance to it. *Recognize you can change people's day in how you talk to them or even how you sell something to them.* Perhaps you feel your day isn't encouraging spirituality. Nonsense. That's only your personal interpretation and limitation. You can bring your own well to anything you do and that is Isaac power that is to be nurtured especially during the afternoon when work is in it's fullest swing and you're most invested in the outside, real world. Be determined to find your way.

In our business day, many things will try to thwart our determination to do the right thing, the godly thing. Take the strength of Isaac and find peace in your determination to bring your special spirit to every part of your life.

Determination to Light the "Fire"

There is a Jewish holiday called Chanukah which is well known to most because it is celebrated by lighting candles in a candelabra known as a menorah. The holiday commemorates the Greek siege on Jerusalem that was overturned by a group of Jewish bandits led by the Macabee family who were able to mobilize forces and regain Jerusalem. Upon reclaiming their land they assessed the damage to the Holy Temple, the most spiritual

Jewish site. They found the interior of the Temple a shambles. They wanted to begin again the spirituality of the Temple by rekindling the golden menorah, an approximate seven foot high candelabra which was to have an eternal flame flickering without pause. However, only the purest oil was allowed to be used in the menorah and it took a seven day process (combined six days of travel and one day of purification) to create this oil ready for the menorah. As they searched through the destruction for a jar of purified oil they stumbled upon one jar of oil, enough to burn for one day, that had not been smashed by the Greeks. It would take an additional seven days to purify oil needed for this service. They rekindled the menorah with the one jar of oil expecting it to last a day and then take a seven day hiatus. Yet, miraculously, it lasted an additional seven days until new purified oil arrived.

Jews celebrate this miracle by lighting the menorah adding a candle each night to symbolize how the miracle grew with every further day the oil lasted. This always struck me as quite an usual Jewish custom because the miracle didn't seem quite as spectacular as so many others described in the Torah and Jewish literature. Yet so much is made of this miracle that it seems me and my fellow Jews can't keep it to ourselves as there is a law that demands the menorah be placed in our windows for all to see. We never do this for all of the other awesome miracles that have happened over the years. Plus, Jewish holidays are always about privacy. Out of respect to God's desire to have unique relationships with everyone as He made them, Judaism severely frowns on attempting to convince others to become Jewish. Jewish holidays are never publicized for the purpose of letting others know all about it.

This miracle however, is different than every other miracle that occurred. Miracles tend to be things that happen around us if not to us. But this miracle was not a God miracle. It was a person-God partnership miracle. After all, a God miracle would have had a fiery ball descend from heaven to light the menorah.

But this miracle was about people who literally wanted to see the "fire" today, immediately even though they had no plan yet for how they'd see the "fire" tomorrow. They showed their Isaac power that day and through sheer determination dug their own "well," and lit that fire. God merely continued their action.

It was wartime. Many people had suffered the loss of loved ones. But these people still searched to see the "fire" and spent the time looking for oil to light that menorah. *They started a miracle by starting to see that fire.*

Isaac power is the devotion during the day when we are not on our own turf, in the comfort of our own choices, to search for the "fire" without thinking about whether or not we'll be successful in the way we plan. It's about sewing spirituality into the fabric of our day instead of seeing it as a separate entity from our employment. That's why the menorah is lit in the window. It is not telling anyone else to be Jewish.

That lit menorah is telling everyone to search for the fire, never stop, never give up the hope of growing your Inner Name and spirituality.

This holiday especially sends this message because the Greeks had outlawed all basic tenets of Judaism. No Sabbath, no circumcision, no learning of Judaic teachings was allowed. So how did the Jews survive their commitment to godliness during this period of oppression? Isaac power. They knew that their godliness didn't depend only on rituals. *Rather, that lifetime commitment to rituals was supposed to imbue in them a passion for godliness that found its way into every aspect of life.* They needed to learn to bring God to the world because they couldn't bring God to their synagogues anymore.

Their devotion to seeing spirituality in every day living, every flower, every smile, every hug, kept them Jewish even without the Jewish traditions. The daytime is for going out into the world and creating a symbiotic relationship between godliness and living every moment.

Isaac did it and now you can do it. Ever hear of a wishing well? Why do you make a wish? Because Isaac got the message across to us over 3500 years ago. Godliness is in that well and that's a great place to connect with your Inner Name, pray and of course, make a wish.

Nighttime

Seeing the Fire in the Dark

The Torah is quoted as calling Jacob a simpleton. This man is anything but simple. He can outmaneuver anyone (although he does struggle and seems to lose to his father-in-law Laban). In fact, he convinces his father that he is his brother Esau in order to attain first born status and receive superior blessing from Isaac. This event follows a spectacular maneuver in which Jacob convinces Esau to sell him the birthright when Esau is hungry and willing to trade it all for a bowl of thick soup. Clearly, Jacob is on a mission throughout his life. He fathers twelve sons that grow to become the twelve tribes of the Jewish people.

The first story that the Torah tells of Jacob alone as the main character is when he is escaping his brother's wrath. After Jacob successfully receives the blessing of Isaac, he knows his brother Esau is angry enough to murder him. He travels toward his Mom's brother, Uncle Laban. But he

Nighttime-Seeing Fire

rests overnight in a field. Before settling for the night, he places many rocks around him in order to protect himself from wild animals. While sleeping, he dreams of angels ascending and descending a ladder stretching up to the heavens. When he awakens, the rocks around him have miraculously melded together to form a pillow under his head. Torah experts explain that the Torah writes that the angels were first ascending. These were the angels that always escorted Jacob. But these angels could only escort him while he was in the land of Israel. Jacob was planning to leave Israel and that is why new escorting angels descended the ladder.

Jacob was indeed a simpleton. But he wasn't simple as in slow in wisdom but rather he had such a clear vision of the "fire" that seeing life from within that fire was simple. He saw angels as real as he saw the people he loved. He saw godliness in everything, even a plain rock. There is a Jewish tradition that explains greater details about that evening. Those rocks began to argue because each one wanted to be under this righteous man's head. Finally as all of the rocks were desperate to do so, they squeezed together forming one stone. Now as much "fire" as I or you may see, I don't envision that when I walk into an auditorium hundreds of chairs begin to argue who should be the one I sit upon. But that's because I'm not Jacob. Because of his clarity, objects came to life for Jacob and everything wanted to be attached to him because being attached to him meant liberating the energy found in every mass as outlined in Einstein's theory of relativity. A rock that once was merely lying in the dirt having little to offer would turn into a holy, godly being that served a purpose in nature when Jacob used it. I know it must sound bizarre to think that objects are thinking and speaking and arguing and I can't say that I believe they do it in such a way that anyone of us could understand. Yet, many of us might feel happy or sad for an object, our car, home, an ancient structure that gets a face lift or is destroyed. Granted we don't believe these objects have brains yet we believe there is some life to them. After all, we think, what have the walls of that structure heard and seen over the years. Science has proven that everything is in some form of motion, the chair you sit on has an atomic structure that is in motion and if liberated would have the energy of itself times the speed of light squared. So although I don't suggest you make a habit of talking to tables, I do suggest that Jacob had the ability to plug in and be sensitive even to objects. Rocks moved for him.

The Torah shows us this example later when Moses is instructed to literally talk to a rock and ask it for water. It is only after Moses hit it with his staff with the prodding of his people that it does yield water and God disallows Moses from bringing the Jews into Israel because he hit the rock instead of continuing to plead with it for water. Spirituality exists in every part of nature and we should learn to have sensitivity to it. It may not feel the same way we feel. A rock doesn't get hot the way you and I do, so we don't have to bring it into the air conditioning but that doesn't mean it doesn't have some form of life and a great purpose that we can recognize and even help it along. After all, mold used to be nothing more than a nuisance. But because Fleming decided to respect it and merely look at the one specimen that for his purposes had been ruined and should have been thrown out, mold gave birth to the single greatest health discovery of that century, anti-biotics. Luckily, he was on a mission and left every possibility open, even ones that first appeared as mistakes.

To better understand Jacob's clarity, consider the story of his "deception" as he pretended to be his brother. The obvious question is why Jacob didn't simply tell his Dad that Esau sold him his birthright. It was the truth. But Jacob, in his simple understanding of life, treasured his father's perspective as well. Even though he knew the blessings of the first born were now his, he would give all of that up so as not to disrupt his father's perspective which was that Esau deserved the blessings. Jacob's vision of godliness is what gave him such extreme respect for other visions and the knowledge that he fit into a greater scheme. Jacob figured it was in God's and Isaac's hands and if Esau received the blessings, so be it. But his Mom, Rebecca, taught Jacob his most valuable lesson about life and God. She explained that he must stand in front of his father and give his father the opportunity to bless him. He'd have to present God with the ability to channel Isaac's blessings to him.

Jacob was not willing to disturb his father's perspective on his brother because his clarity and "simple" nature showed him there were so many other unique ways to see the "fire." Who was he to explain anything to his righteous and powerful father? Instead he presented himself to Isaac in a combination of both he and his brother and allowed Isaac to decide. Isaac recites the famous words, "your arms are the arms of Esau (Esau had hairy arms so Rebecca placed some hairy animal skins on

Jacob's arms) but your voice is the voice of Jacob." Clearly, Jacob being Esau's twin could have mimicked the voice of Esau. But commentaries explain that Isaac wasn't referring to the voice pattern but the speech pattern. Jacob spoke to his father with a respect that Esau never did. Again, if Jacob's intention was to fool his Dad, he could've just said things exactly how he knew Esau would have said them. But his purpose was not to get the blessings but merely present a situation where he could. At this point, Isaac could've stood up and said, "Hey, hold it one minute here, something screwy is going on here. He feels like Esau, speaks like Jacob. I'm blind, let me call my wife in here and get to the bottom of this." But instead Isaac smells the spiritual fragrance of the heavenly world to come and knows that whomever is in front of him is deserving of these powerful blessings. Jacob must maneuver but not disturb Isaac's perspective. Rather he presents a situation where Isaac can on his own choose to change his perspective. That is incredible integrity, honesty, clarity of life and spirituality.

Jacob has the clearest vision of spirituality of the three patriarchs. It is why he institutes his prayer at night when he feels clarity is at its height. At night we can see what is called in Hebrew the "emmes," the truth. Nighttime is when the charge of the world and its craziness slows. The world stops functioning with the hustle and bustle of daytime. Until recently you couldn't even get around too well at night. It's darkness provides us with a call to ponder and contemplate, leading us to soul searching thoughts and spiritual answers of godliness. It is a wise time to remember our priorities in the quiet of our souls. Frankly, it can be a scary time as well because we stop, we get tired, we quiet down and are left with primarily ourselves.

The one antidote to calm contemplation has become television. People have found the method to never stop and think quietly about life and goals for tomorrow. In order to find the simple truth in the night we have to provide ourselves with some alone time.

◆*Exercise*◆

Create 15 minutes of quiet time in the night (after the kids are asleep if necessary) and use this time to be alone (walking in your neighborhood might help) thinking, reviewing your day and considering what you will do tomorrow to bring Abraham's kindness to others and Isaac's power to yourself. Create a list in your mind of two items for each. Then spend three to five minutes in the dark, eyes open or closed as you soulbreathe and connect with your Inner Name. Finally, step outside and gaze at the moon and ask yourself how you are different today than last night and how you'd like to be different tomorrow. As you use nighttime to strengthen your clarity, you'll see every part of your day change and you'll find greater clarity in all parts of your life.

Part Three: How You Will Change the World and Everyone In It

One Moment-One Action-Changes the World Forever

There are countless examples of how one action forever changed the course of history or changed a person's life or a family or community which again, in turn, changes history forever. Because we are godly, immortal beings, we prove our power daily whenever we choose to. Only godly beings, partners with God could make such a difference to another and to the world. After all, we are small people living in our tiny piece of this planet. But our souls and hearts can encompass the universe with our love and determination to see "fire." Out of every story I've read, heard or experienced, there is a Biblical story that serves as my personal inspiration for this power of the moment and the ripple effect it has on life. Oddly, you probably don't know the name of my small hero which is a primary reason why he is so intriguing-a literal nobody like you and me-who changed history again and again.

This man was anything but a hero. We don't know much about him and there's seemingly only one noteworthy thing he did. I'm not sure it's nearly as incredible as so many other inspiring Biblical stories. But this one individual stood among millions of people frozen in fear as they faced most certain pain and probable death. No one took action. No one knew what to do. The most powerful army known to humankind was charging angrily at them. These broken men, the culmination of generations of slaves, had just escaped Egypt due solely to the strength of this powerful God they only recently began to reconnect with. They were leaving after ten horrific plagues destroyed much of Egypt's spirit. And now they were stuck with a sea in front of them and nothing less than an insanely angry mob of an army charging toward them. They had been in slavery for 210 years and had no intention of fighting their slave masters. Even the great, masterful Moses stood waiting. Apparently this sudden attack wasn't in Moses' plan book.

People began to complain to Moses. They couldn't understand why they went through all of this saving, the drama of the escape, to be murdered there in the outskirts of Egypt. It was perhaps the tensest moment in Biblical history. Then an extraordinary thing happened. One person, no more special than the next, did something. He stood and began to walk into the great Red Sea. He captured the vision of the people as he simply walked into the water undisturbed continuing until the water reached his nostrils. At that point he looked skyward and uttered a Hebrew phrase that every Jewish prayer book contains as part of its daily liturgy. Mi Chamocha BaAlim Hashem… Who is like you God… too awesome to praise. Suddenly, God informs Moses to spread his staff and the sea splits, offering a safe exit for the Jewish people and the beginning of their nationhood.

This man did something that changed the course of history. He understood the concept of being a partner with God. Everyone else, including Moses, awaited something from God. This man knew he could change God, begin a miracle, walk into that water, the only escape route he could figure and *offer God an idea* for an exit. Who knows what would have happened had this man not walked into that water? Perhaps the Jews would have fought and lost many lives that day. Perhaps God would have saved them with some other miracle, like floating them over the sea. Yet, the splitting of the Red Sea is without a doubt the most well known Biblical miracle and story and it all began because of one man whose name you never knew until now, *Nachshone*. He didn't even know what he was doing. Listen to his words. He didn't have the confidence of an Abraham or Moses to say something like, "Respectfully, God, to kill us here will make others believe you are weak…" or "Reconsider and give us a chance to repent…"

No, he just feels with his soul and prays as a humble unknown. His words are telling, "Who is like you...Too awesome to praise..." Nachshone is sending the message of a young child. "I don't begin to understand you, your world. I haven't begun to see the 'fire.' But I know you are my father and I love You and am in awe of Your love and devotion to your children. I can't begin to formulate a real PR campaign here and offer any real suggestion. I can only let you know that I am here believing in my Inner Name, ready to develop my godliness and bring it to the world. If you let me, although it's hard for me to imagine, I will be Your partner and I will walk into the depths of any ocean if that means walking hand in hand with You."

Nachshone is and will always be my hero. He is the hero of every one of us who don't have it all together, don't have the answers, have many days when we don't see the "fire" so clearly. He empowers every one of us. He taught us that we don't have to wait to become an Abraham or Moses to speak to God, to make seas split, to make the world stand up and take notice, to change the course of history. We don't have to have a plan, be in the inner circle, have great spiritual knowledge that others don't, to make a difference by being His partner. Just by feeling soulful all of us can be a *Nachshone*, asking God to help even if we can't formulate a reason why or are lost and just want to say, "Hey, Dad, I love you and need your help." That is a genuine love that God relates to more than anything else. It is that love that Nachshone tapped into and began the greatest miracle in human history.

God always presents each of us with seemingly strange situations that may not seem to have much rhyme or reason. But He is always giving us opportunities to step up to the plate and take our best swing to change our little piece of the world. We are constantly being offered moments to emerge as a hero or heroine of our story. If we are like Nachshone, we'll write our own story of inspiring godliness. Be the person who wants to take the swing even though you might strike out. Don't offer that moment of heroism to anyone else. Grab it and be that hero to your world.

But Wait There's More

Approximately 120 years later…

A woman who was an Egyptian princess gave away everything: family ties, fame and fortune to pursue a dream. Her husband had died, his wealth gone leaving her penniless and childless. All she had was an aged mother-in-law who needed her help. This woman could have easily chosen to do as her sister did, return to her father and be welcomed with a lifetime of riches. But this woman sought something else. This mother-in-law intrigued her. This aged woman had something she'd never seen before; a spirit, a godliness within that just flowed with the ease like that of water from a pitcher. This meant more to her than all of the riches in the world.

She fell in love with this old woman, fell in love with her godliness and uttered famous words to express her devotion.

"Where you go, I will go. Your people are my people. Where you will be buried I will be buried." Her name was Ruth and she was able to see the "fire" through her connection to Naomi, her mother-in-law. Ruth converts to Judaism and returns to Israel with Naomi, even though they are forced to subsist on the charity of others. Ruth spends days in the warm fields during harvesting awaiting some preciously needed grain to be left behind so that she could use it for herself and her mother-in-law. This was the one of the charitable laws in Israeli society at the time. Through Divine work behind the scenes, Ruth is introduced to Boaz, a wealthy, spiritual, distant cousin of Naomi. She wants this 80 year old man to marry her daughter-in-law and thus renew her family name in Israel. (Naomi's husband and two sons died. Judaic teaching faults them for their unwillingness to share their wealth with those who were needy).

Boaz is sympathetic to his distant cousin and finds Ruth extremely spiritual and modest. Even the way she picks up the grain from the field catches his eye. She bends her knees down instead of bending over as a gesture of modesty. But, Boaz adhering to the law of that time-that the next closest relative to a man who passes is to marry his childless wife, knows of another cousin who is more closely related than he. The other cousin is approached to see if he wants to marry Ruth and carry out his obligation to have a child with her and continue the name of his deceased cousin. Yet, this man refuses. He cites a Jewish law stating that a Jew could never marry anyone from the tribe of Moab. The Moabites had tried to kill the Jews when they were in need of kindness from the Moabites in the desert. Due to that indecency, a law was passed that even if a Moabite converted to Judaism; still, a Jew couldn't marry that individual. This other relative passes on marrying Ruth. Boaz was a spiritual leader in Israel and interpreter of the laws and he believed differently. He explained that the law only referred to Moabite men because it was the men who tried to murder the Jews, not the women. He declared that if a Moabite woman became Jewish, any Jew could indeed marry her. Based on this interpretation of the law, Boaz does marry her.

Try to imagine the scene. Boaz is an eighty-year old man, known for his spiritual leadership throughout the land. He knows that he's done his good for society and could probably just coast to the end of his days. He surely doesn't want to rock the boat and take a chance that everything he's worked for be reversed in any way. This "Ruth the Moabite" question became a serious debate. One that Boaz would have been safe to say, "Maybe you're right, I won't marry her." The Jewish law didn't demand he marry her. Everyone agreed that he could refuse with no penalty but Ruth would not have a baby to name after her deceased husband from a man in her husband's family, she wouldn't be able to carry on her husband's Inner Name. Boaz takes a remarkable chance. If he is wrong, he'll lose his status and reputation as a spiritual leader. To say "no" is the safest and seemingly smartest thing to do. But Boaz says "yes." Boaz is not interested in *coasting* to his death. He is on a constant spiritual search for growth of any kind. He realizes this situation came to him from God and he fights with whomever he needs to in order to do what he believes is the right thing. He takes his spiritual swing at the plate with bases loaded and hits a grand slam.

Boaz marries Ruth, sleeps with her one night, impregnates her and dies the following day. He was one day away from death and his greatest spiritual journey and quest had yet to occur. Ruth gave birth from her union with Boaz and the great grandson of the this couple is none other than King David, one of the most powerful and spiritual people ever in history and the believed progenitor of the eventual Jewish messiah. Boaz searches and finds immortality. As great as he was, none of us would have known who he was. Only because of his last stand for inner godliness did he make his inner name great. But where did Boaz learn this strength to search for godliness and boldly step up to the plate and make things happen? Boaz was none other than the grandson of *Nachshone*, the very man who got the ball rolling at the Red Sea.

But Wait There's More...

Almost 1,100 years later, as discussed above, the Greek empire and the Jewish nation were in a vicious battle in Jerusalem as the Greek empire wished to destroy the Jews, their laws and traditions and their Holy Temple. The Greek empire was able to overtake Jerusalem eventually and even destroy the inside of the Holy Temple. But the battles still continued with a band of Jewish militia men that had been growing and training in the foothills of Jerusalem. This militia was led by the Maccabee brothers who were gaining strength as the days wore on. The battles were personally tragic for the Maccabee family as only one brother survived the battles and went on to lead the Jewish people after miraculously defeating the professional and powerful armies of the Greek empire. The Macabees had multiple chances to throw in the towel. They suffered great losses to their militia and never did anyone believe they could win without God's intervention. But the Maccabbees kept their strength and belief because they knew they had to create a partnership with God. They knew they couldn't wait for God to hand them victory on a silver platter. They'd have to show God their land was worth fighting for and even dying for. Was it a coincidence that this family took the lead in the fight for their nation's and religion's survival? Not at all. In fact they learned well from their ancestor how to go forward even when all of the answers aren't yet clear. And they made this search for godliness their Inner Name, literally. Because the name Maccabee is a Hebrew (it only bears four letters in Hebrew) acronym for the first four spiritual words uttered by Nachshone when the sea had reach his nostrils, "*M*i *C*homocha *B*aalim *H*ashem" (It doesn't translate well but believe me that the first four letters of the first four words of that phrase are the only four letters that make up the Macabee name in Hebrew).

One action by one man not only changes the course of history at that moment, saving the lives of millions of people but serves as an inspiration to generations to come who draw on it to search for greater godliness in their lives. And now, you and I can be inspired by *Nachshone* as well and develop identities full of searching for godliness and going forward in areas that we believe in. The wait is over. Our history is in our hands. We'll make of it as we choose with our godliness.

Individuals Who Formed a New Country of New Freedom

This past year, I studied the American revolution with my family (we're homschoolers) and found so many inspiring stories. I learned of men who lived their whole lives but because of one action, one phrase, one deciding moment, they achieved immortality and offered others lifetimes of inspiration. It reinforced my understanding that each of us has to keep searching to see the "fire" more and more until the day we die because we never know what our most splendid spiritual moment will be. Boaz is not known for a lifetime of spirituality but for the best decision of his life moments before his death.

Nathan Hale, a patriot spy, is known for one statement which he said before he was hung by the British, "I regret that I have but one life to give for my country." His last words served as empowerment to so many others who would fight to the death for freedom. John Hancock used to practice his signature as a child always believing his signature would be famous one day. Well, imagine that his name is used as a term referring to a signature-just put your John Hancock right there. You may not know much more about him and there's a lot to know. But it is his signature, which only took a moment of his life to write but a lifetime of work to make it meaningful that inspires us today. Paul Revere had made many messenger runs to save lives but it was his one midnight ride that was immortalized in Longfellow's poem. That midnight ride gave patriots time to move the no longer secret place where the arms were held and time to move Sam Adams and John Hancock to avoid what would have otherwise been their most certain death. The revolution would probably been instantly crushed that night if not for a brave forty year old man who had already spent most of his life trying to help the cause.

Patrick Henry was another man of strong beliefs. He gave voice to the feelings of men unwilling to live a life without liberty. One quote made him famous and immortal, "Give me liberty or give me death." These men searched to bring their beliefs to fruition and stuck by those beliefs in the face of extreme danger. Individuals are powerful. Our country won it's independence because of the masses who fought for what they believed in but the inspiration came from individuals who earnestly sought their Inner Name and maintained their beliefs with honesty and integrity at all costs.

An example of this belief in a new system of freedom at any cost was exemplified by a favorite story of mine about Samuel Adams. He was a leader in Boston and quite a trouble maker. He was known to stir crowds into passionate rebellions, sometimes even leading to the tar and feathering of British troops. But what I respect him most for is a story about maintaining his beliefs. After the Boston massacre which wasn't a massacre at all, the British troops were being held for trial. Now Sam was one of the people who purposely tried and succeeded in making the Boston massacre sound much worse than it was. Even today, most people think hundreds of people were murdered by British troops when in fact it's believed that only 7 patriots were killed-this was only after a patriot mob was throwing snowballs with brick pieces cleverly hidden in them at British troops. Yet, Sam Adams, with all of his hate and disgust for Britain, did something remarkable-he maintained his beliefs. Knowing that the troops could never get a fair trial he pleaded repeatedly (Sam was known to be a difficult person so his cousin really wanted nothing to do with him and surely nothing to do with defending British troops) with his cousin, John Adams to defend the troops. Sam believed in his cause for freedom and never allowed that belief to sway even if it meant helping his enemy. His cousin did a fine job defending them. The troops were freed after trial.

Can you imagine how many individuals left their mark through their own personal godliness and made a difference to others? All of us are individuals who have the energy of thirty huge hydrogen bombs. You and I can liberate that energy when we search and find our Inner Name and godliness.

Love Thy Neighbor As Thyself

In order to make a difference you have to believe in yourself. When the Torah demands that all of us love our neighbors as ourselves it commits us to loving two people, our neighbor *and* ourselves. Being a psychotherapist, I know plenty of people who don't like themselves at all nor do they treat themselves kindly. To them I'd say, please don't treat your neighbor like you treat yourself. Just love your neighbor even though you can't stand yourself deep down. But of course the Torah wants us; no, *demands* that all of us love ourselves. Why such a demand? People have told me with an obvious tone in their voice, "You can't love another until you love yourself." To which I've responded with,

"Why not?" I know people who don't love themselves and yet they're kind and loving to their children or seem to be. I usually get a puzzled look in return to my "why not?" as if to say that I'm questioning something so obvious I must not be astute enough to understand the principal so it's not worth trying to explain it to me.

I've discovered the answer to my question over time (perhaps it was simple to others but I needed time to discover it for myself). One incident started me on my way to my personal answers. Over the years, I've helped parents learn to talk to their kids in such a way that helps their children feel understood. It's a concept known by many therapists, referred to as "active listening." The idea is to simply respond to your child with the heart of their message and the feeling that you hear in their voice. For example, when Allison tells Mommy that she hasn't seen Daddy for a long time and wants to see him, Mommy could respond with, "It sounds like you're sad that Daddy isn't around and you

Love Thy Neighbor as Thyself

want to know when you'll see him next." One night in one of my workshops, I was helping parents learn this technique. Each parent was taking turns using the active listening responses when one woman said a perfectly worded response. It flowed from her mouth so smoothly. Everyone stared, jaws collectively fell to the floor. Not because she had gotten it so right but because she said it so beautifully and yet it sounded so cold, so devoid of love and emotion. I learned that night that teaching a loving response by teaching how to say certain words was pointless.

What is love? It is far deeper than doing the right things for people. Many people can be kind and appropriate to others. They can provide actions that a loving person would provide but that doesn't mean they're providing love. Many adults tell me that when they were kids, their parents provided them with loving actions-made sure they had food and clothing, cared for them when they were sick, made birthday parties for them, made sure they received the best schooling and kept on top of them scholastically- but never felt like their parents "got them." That's not something you learn from a seminar or provide by using fancy words or newfangled parenting techniques. Offering love comes from a feeling of love within. We draw on inner love to offer love no different than having to obtain knowledge before teaching it. We may learn to love even more through the experience of loving others the same way we might understand information even better through teaching it. But you still must posses love in order to spread it around. If you don't love yourself, you don't have love in your actions, just a smart mind that tells you what you should be doing. Of course it's not all or nothing. So someone can love herself somewhat and show love to her kids somewhat. *But there's no doubt that the more someone loves herself, the more feelings of love will be wrapped up in every loving action.*

Loving your neighbor as yourself is explaining that real love comes through connection to yourself that you then extend to others. Why do we love our children more than anything? Because we see them as an extensions of ourselves. How do we truly love others? By feeling so connected that we see them as extensions of ourselves. As we grow more peaceful within and discover more inner love, we can be truly loving to others the more we see them as parts of ourselves. When your arm gets a new watch, your finger, a new ring, your neck, a necklace, your upper body, a new shirt; your legs don't get jealous and complain. As a whole body you're happy because the ultimate goal is the entire body. When you see godliness within everyone, you begin to realize how much all of us are connected to each other through our godliness and how we are part of one body, one soul, one God.

Love your neighbor as yourself is telling you that your neighbor is *yourself so do everything you can to enhance her or else your entire body is going to be minimized.*

Real love comes from one part of you, your soul. It is your only immortal part, the part that can touch another and change our world. Without it you're an aging animal counting her days to eventual doom. With it, you have the immortality and invincibility of God.

This is why love is timeless. You can love people instantly and love them years after they've passed on. Because once our souls connect, we're on Godly time and that is beyond our feeble measurement of time. Love comes from our own personal connection with our Inner Name. And that is ultimately where our self-esteem and feeling of deserving of self-love emanates.

The first step of loving your neighbor as yourself is loving yourself. The second step is allowing yourself to connect and see others as an extension of yourself.

Allowing Yourself to Connect and See Others as Yourself

Once you begin to love yourself in a whole new meaningful way, you'll begin to see how connected you can be to everyone else. Jealousy comes from a lack of peace within yourself. If you feel you've got it all, you don't have to envy anyone else. You can look at others and say, "I want that for myself," without wishing that they didn't have it. You can *learn* from others, there are better ways of living that you might want to tap into and use others as a model. But the moment you start to feel jealous you must remind yourself that you're feeling "less than" and malcontent within. This jealousy is declaring to you that you don't really see the "fire" inside you and are not finding the inner peace because you're not recognizing your Inner Name, your power and the partnership you have with God. You're dying a little at a time-you've forgotten how to live. You need to get back to the basics of your godliness and find spiritual pursuits.

If you saw your neighbor as an extension of yourself, part of the godly team that is needed to keep developing God's master plan for the world, then jealousy would have no role in your life. We aren't jealous (or surely are significantly less jealous) if our children have something that we don't. Again, we feel that they are an extension of ourselves not much different than a part of our own bodies and therefore find their accomplishments a part of our own. That's true of your neighbor as well. She is a part of the partnership in this world and is needed to do her part. It's not for you to agree or disagree on how she develops her Inner Name because you are not chairman of board but just a board member. You can make suggestions or try to develop a partnership with that board member but each of you has your own purpose and you desperately need each other to accomplish your goals. Now this is where it's hard for people to have vision. We've become so individualized that we don't see how anyone else is really necessary to our personal spiritual goals. We forget the basics... We need others for everything, to help us live. We need others to help feed, shelter, and clothe us. We forget that a common CEO who may make twenty times our salary is necessary in some way toward our own ability to create income or live in some other way (if not just to keep our economy humming). We forget that the migrant worker who plucks fruits off a tree is necessary to help us have food for strength so that we can focus on our inner name.

When is the last time you stopped during a road backup and rolled down your window and said "thank you" or any kind word to the man who's fixing your street in the heat of the day? Why not? He's working at something which helps you. Even if it doesn't help you directly it may help your aging grandma one day when she drives to visit you and will have a wider, safer street. When you think of people in this way, there is no end to your thankfulness for others. There is no end to the partnership you can feel with the rest of the world.

Instead of seeing others as competitors in life, see them as extensions of yourself-love them with the love you have within-see the spirituality they offer by doing things that can help so many others. It doesn't matter if they do it just for a paycheck or to help others as well.

Your life is profoundly different because of them and their efforts offer you greater energy to do special things. Now if you choose to take life and create a vibrant "fire" within then everything anyone else has ever done for you directly or indirectly has a spiritual gain. Their connection and Inner Name has deepened because they're a part of helping you with your spiritual endeavor whether they're aware of it or not. With every spiritual moment you have, you connect yourself to all of those who have ever helped you in your spiritual quest, from the man who collects your garbage (that saves you a lot of heartache and time) to the composer of the beautiful music you listen to in order to relax or dance with your partner. If you choose to take your life and

Love Thy Neighbor as Thyself

indulge in a way that does not develop your Inner Name, you've diminished all of the work everyone else has done in this world. They've merely offered you luxury toward no end or betterment of life. Those who've died to offer you freedom gave their lives so that either you could better your godliness or be merely self indulgent with no concern for anyone or anything else. You (along with others of course) will decide which one they gave their lives for.

In the movie, *Saving Private Ryan*, Tom Hanks' character is dying as a direct result of trying to save the private. Before death he looks at the private and says, "Make it count." This common person gave his life for this stranger and whether or not that sacrifice was worth it depended on what Private Ryan was going to choose to do with the rest of his life. You will decide whether the efforts of others were worthwhile or not. Keep that in mind when your work at your own job. Why collect a paycheck when you can be changing the world at the same time. Take your job seriously and do the best you possibly can at it. Don't reduce your job to just getting ahead or keeping it. Make your job about living a spiritual life by helping the world in your own way. There is no job that can't help and most that are quite necessary to the betterment of this world.

Why stop here? You can love more than just your neighbor as thyself. Consider what nature has done for you. The trees that oxygenate your air; you couldn't breathe without them. The ground and animals that offer you their food, the pets that offer you love, the sun that offers you light and vitamin C (you absorb vitamins from different parts of the atmosphere). You are a partner with everything in nature. And again, if you choose to pursue your Inner Name, you offer spirituality to every part of your ecosystem. But if not, then that animal who gave her life for you, didn't die with much purpose. You make the decision. Life becomes full of happiness and togetherness when you can see deeper into yourself. If you are feeling distant from others, do something to bring them closer to you. Help them in some way that can make you feel connected-that they are a part of you-an extension of your world-and then you can love their success and what they've done for the world and for you.

Love is endless and spiritual. And that is why it is one of the most beautiful ways to focus on your spirituality. When you gaze at your child, for instance, there is no explanation for the overwhelming feeling you have. The safety felt when you were younger in your parents' arms is beyond this world. The intense love you may have for your spouse after only knowing her for a relatively short time is godly. The more you focus on the feelings of love in these relationships, the more godliness you'll have in your life. Every moment you focus on love is another moment of connecting to your immortal self.

One of the important ways to develop these relationships and your own Inner Name is to bring your unique spirit to each of these love relationships.

Our love is deepened when we build our love through our souls. Unfortunately, too many of our meaningful relationships are shortchanged because we aren't trying to tap into our spirituality in the context of the relationship.

> Ask yourself:
> What is the meaning of my marriage?
> What is the meaning of my parent-child bond?
> What is the purpose of each of these relationships?

These are ambiguous questions and no two people could answer them exactly the same. But most people are never considering the questions. We aren't trained to see or consider the deeper spiritual picture and are in danger of our most spiritual relationships being reduced to making money, paying bills, having laughs, decent sex, doing some good for others… When it comes to our children many parents rarely consider why they have children. They probably have a vision for what kind

Love Thy Neighbor as Thyself 213

of future they want for their child but it usually surrounds the child's personal happiness which usually gets back to money, having laughs... It seems that being happy has been translated to drinking and dancing, letting yourself go like when you were in college (for those who let themselves go in this way in college). I'll never forget this huge block party I attended when I was on a vacation in Key West where everyone was dancing with alcohol in the streets (yes I meant dancing with alcohol, it appeared as though many of them weren't aware of whether they were dancing with a partner or not). This was fun? This was escape from unhappy times. If life has become so consistently sour that the thought of drinking and "letting go" is something to look forward to with consistency, consider how to change your life instead of running from it.

All of us need to discover why we have children, spouses, friends... If we don't know then begin considering some meaningful answers. Start by interacting with your loved ones through meaningful pursuits. Create a relationship with your spouse that surrounds spirituality, taking time together to do for others for example. Recently, I was helping a childless couple develop a healthier marriage. They expected to depend on a child to keep them busy and create their marriage. Now they only had each other. They tried filling their time with "fun"-bowling, bike riding, dinners. But they needed much more to keep the relationship strong. They needed a deeper reason to be in love. They had to find a spiritual togetherness that gave them new definition to their marriage, something they could bring to each other. They began taking their Sundays (yes, their day off) and visiting hospital patients together as a couple. They still went bowling but now they occasionally took a neighbor's child whose sibling was severely mentally challenged so this child could experience a little extra friendship. They began discussing philosophy about life and spirituality (something they thought neither wanted to do until it was brought up in a session) and began to know each other on a whole new plane. They made their marriage into a meaningful relationship and became strong partners because they were connecting through their souls.

Consider what spirituality is brought into your marital relationship. Begin talking with your spouse about some activities that are meaningful to each of you and plan to do them together. The closeness you'll feel will amaze you. Godliness is powerful and all it takes is a little focus from you, God does the rest.

This principle is the same for your children. It isn't enough to take care of our kids and make sure they're fed, clothed, hugged and educated. Your truest relationship with your child depends on the spirituality you and your child bring to it. Participate together in meaningful pursuits that either help others or engage your child in the miracles of our lives. Planting a garden is miraculous and you and your child start the miracle with every seed planted. Visiting kids in the hospital, making sandwiches for the homeless, giving out flowers to residents at the nursing home, baking an apple pie for a neighbor all help you and your child relate on a spiritual level and this bond is stronger than any other. You offer your child meaningful reasons to be alive and a world full of miracles to focus on and draw strength from time and again. Plus, you give your child incredible self-esteem as she sees that she can make a difference even at a young age. Any child feels ten feet tall when he sees others so appreciative of his actions. This will cause your child to always search for activities that will make him feel that way, that spiritual value. Your bond with your child will change immediately and it's never too late to start, even if your child is an adult. The love between two people and a family that is based on spirituality is one that exists forever and is ever developing. This love feeds our self-value proving our godliness again and again as we connect with the souls of our many loved ones.

I could talk about love forever because it is what my life begins and ends with. The most fascinating part about loving others is that ultimately it helps us to love God as we connect more and more to His creations. God is omnipotent and you can't reach out and touch Him, kiss Him, talk to Him and love Him. But you can in a way because He has given us treasures, pieces of Himself in every person, flower, animal, in every cell that makes up our world. If we can see the "fire" and love all of these parts of God, then we are falling in love with God Himself. We can touch Him in the dirt that we plant in, kiss Him on the cheeks of our children and hug Him in the arms of our partner. If we see the "fire," then God will be in the midst of it as clearly as when Moses saw godliness in the burning bush.

Loving Yourself

The entire crux of this book is to open your eyes to the "fire" that burns inside you. Every soulful breath, kind gesture, three patriarchal day is the avenue by which you can find and nurture your Inner Name. This is your self-value. Unfortunately, self-value in today's society has become intertwined with money, fame and power-they are the ones who "have." Those who got it are supposed to feel really special within and those who don't-the have nots-believe they'd feel special if only they had it. For some reason, the multitude of stories of those who have it all and are divorced, heartbroken, distant from their loved ones and substance abusers aren't enough to convince many of the have nots that happiness in life isn't about any of those things. Self-value is about a feeling within, not an outside system of proving your value to yourself. The more you define your godliness the greater self-value you'll have. What greater meaning can you have in

Loving Yourself 219

life than to be connected to your immortal godly self?

Inner peace is the domain of anyone. But it doesn't find you. You have to find it. You have to adjust your focus so that you can see the "fire" everyday, at work and at play, in every relationship. Whenever I talk of self-value, I have to remind you that so many people are tearing themselves down because they unconsciously are using the messages they received in childhood to dictate their sense of self. I go into great depths in my books on marriage and relationships and raising children of divorce to help people understand that connection and then, if necessary, turn it around.

Imagine if you will a five-year-old little girl who offers her Dad (who hasn't smoked for months) the requisite ugly green and orange misshapen ash tray as a Father's Day present. Dad looks down at his little girl and says, "Oh my gosh! You made this all by yourself? It's incredible. Look honey (motioning to his wife) can you believe this? I have to put this right in the middle of my desk at the office first thing tomorrow." How does that little girl feel? She can't feel any more wonderful. She believes she is great, extremely talented, and has the power to make a difference to her surroundings. Now the truth is she made an ugly misshapen ash tray only a father could love but "truth" doesn't reflect her feelings. Dad is pleased and she has pleased him. She feels fantastic about herself.

Now imagine the same scenario but this time Dad shrugs and says through a smirk, "Well, it's kinda nice and all but I haven't smoked for a long time." That same girl with the same ash tray feels absolutely dejected. That one incident isn't going to shape her life but the consistency of either message is going to have an indelible impact on how she sees herself. Most often, parents don't mean to do anything but send love to their kids and they try hard but they aren't perfect and as such make mistakes. They send messages without ever realizing it. Their own diminished self-esteem could lie at the heart of why they don't emotionally understand their kid. Depression, financial issues, marital discord could all lie behind a parent's neglect of a child. How we are treated as kids gives us our first impression of who we are. We navigate life continuously based on how we came to understand our self-value.

Now as adults it's crucial to recognize what were the underlying messages of our youth and be determined to redefine ourselves based on who we've become today, not based on the impressions we were given by our parents for better or for worse. You wouldn't want to continue to see yourself as less than even though you do so much for others because your upbringing gave you to believe you weren't so special. Likewise, you wouldn't want to see yourself as a fabulous person becoming self indulgent and not giving much to others because your childhood led you to believe you were fantastic and didn't need to do anything to be so. Now as an adult at any age, it is your decision to judge what makes you a person of self-value, your belief. Many of my patients are quite surprised that I don't take what seems to be the expected psychobabble approach to self-esteem-you're wonderful because of who you are. That's a crock! I tell my patients to get some self-esteem. They create a list of things that they feel would make them special and if they don't have enough there then they better get out and do something that gives them a sense of value. If they already do plenty that should make them feel valuable then they have to grow up and recognize they're allowing their childhood impressions to determine their sense of self and that's not fair. They'll have to judge themselves based on who they are every day. If they aren't happy with who they are every day then they can change that too. The power is in your hands.

♦*Exercise* ♦

Create a list of what makes you special-not more special than others-just special. Review that list. If your friend gave you this list would you say she should feel special? If the answer is yes, then recognize you are no less than your friend and deserve to feel special. You might have to fight some childhood impressions to get where you belong. For the next week, stop yourself before every meal (it's just a set time to use rather than setting an alarm) and take out this list and remind yourself how special you're allowed and supposed to feel. Give yourself permission to feel godly.

However, if your list reveals that you are not special (even if your friend showed you the same list, you wouldn't tell her that she should feel special) write five things more that you could do or focus on that would help you feel special. In either case, write next to each item on your list how you can do each item in a more spiritual way. Then put that into practice.

So much of what we do is based on childhood. Statistically, we end up close to living as our parents did-sharing the same moral and ethical beliefs, similar type of marriage, similar work ethic... I know you may say that's absurd but if you really let yourself consider this, you'll see most people aren't like apples and oranges when it comes to the similarities they share with their parents. And there is a reason of course that God put you in the hands of the parents that you had, for better or for worse; to teach you some powerful lessons and be able to develop into an individual who has her power to change the world in her own unique way.

Well, it's time to unleash your atomic energy, your spiritual self on the world with no agenda other than to connect within your own self and love yourself like you've never loved yourself before. You are a dynamic chip off the old block and God is the old block. You are partners with the entire world forevermore. Now take that and learn to practice a life full of "fire" and you'll see what true love is. Take one minute at each meal to just think about how great you are because of what you're capable of. Even if you haven't achieved what you deem as greatness, it's the knowledge that you have the opportunity to do special things that empowers you. I feel I have so much more to do to give of myself here on this world. But I'm not sad that I haven't done it, I'm excited about making it happen and watching how God as my partner will allow it all to unfold. My life is like a compelling movie (to me at least) and I'm sitting on the edge of my seat in anticipation of what will happen next. The knowledge that I can and will make a difference even though I know it won't go exactly according to my plans is wonderful and I love myself, God and this life because of it. Ultimately, what does make you special? It is those actions, thoughts and feelings that tie you into your spiritual self.

Prayer

As you realize that God is not esoteric and very much a regular, real part of your life, you can begin to understand why prayer is so important.

Prayer is one of our most direct ways to talk to God. It's a beautiful method because it helps us realize that God is right here with us, willing and able to listen. Unfortunately, religions have often made prayer so regular that it challenges many to feel that they are communicating their own personal prayers. Some religious institutions do a great job of singing prayers together as a congregation and encouraging everyone to create unique prayers. But for many, these prayers seem stale and fixed. Don't be dissuaded by anyone else's interpretation of prayer or comments on how you should do it. The important thing is that you feel God is real enough to simply talk to.

It was a pregnant woman by the name of Hannah that taught us how to pray. Around 931 B.C.E. the Jewish high priest Eli, saw this woman sitting and talking to herself. Convinced that she was drunk, Eli began to scold her. But Hannah explained that she was merely praying and felt that God was so close and so real to her that she felt it normal to say real words to Him no different than if she were to speak to anyone. Eli marveled at her innate understanding and taught every person thereafter to pray through the same speech as they'd use to communicate with anyone else. Hannah had been praying that she should give birth to a child who was ripe to see the "fire" and be godly. She was the mother of none other than Samuel the prophet.

Amazingly, prayer seems to have incredible powers, even healing powers as discussed in one major study. There had been many positive studies that discovered that patients who prayed or were prayed for and knew about the prayers healed faster and better. But one study wanted to see what would happen if people prayed for patients who did not know anyone was praying for them. In a randomized, double-bind study, over a twelve month period, nine hundred and ninety consecutive patients admitted to the Mid America Heart Institute in Kansas City, Missouri, were sorted into two groups.

One group received Intercessory prayer (someone prayed for them) and the other group did not. The 75 intercessors, who never met the patients, were drawn from different denominations in the local community but all agreed with the statement: "I believe in God. I believe He is personal and is concerned with individual lives. I further believe that He is responsive to prayers for healing made on behalf of the sick." The intercessors were asked to pray daily for 28 days for a "speedy recovery with no complications." None of the patients knew about the existence of the study.

Using the patients' coronary care unit scores, members of the prayer group fared 11% better than those who weren't prayed for. These results were published on October 25, 1999, in the science journal The Archives of Internal Medicine (there is another similar study where 5 people prayed for 466 patients at the St. Luke's Hospital in Kansas City and the patients needed less medication and recovered faster). The list of studies that discuss how faith is helpful to our physical selves goes on and on. For example, greater religious involvement has been associated with lower blood pressure, fewer strokes, lower rates of death from heart disease, lower mortality after heart surgery and longer survival in general. Hospital stays are nearly two and a half times longer for older patients who don't have a religious affiliation. People who are more religious experience less depression, anxiety, and are less likely to commit suicide. Then there are real creative studies that prove that prayer helped speed seed germination and that negative prayer halted germination-yet another study that indicated that prayer affected microorganism growth in Petri dishes. But these studies will never convince anyone about your godliness. You could always find ways to explain them away and I am often skeptical of studies myself. These prayer studies merely give you yet another glimpse into how much godliness is awaiting all of us who want to see the "fire."

Prayer is one simple form of connecting to our Inner Name and realizing that there is spirituality everywhere at every moment. Learn to find comfort in talking to God at any time. But make it real-to you. In other words, it's not for me to say that you should start off your prayer to God with, "Oh great holy one" or "How are You?" because it depends on your genuine Inner Name and the relationship you are ever developing with God. But at least create a minimum of once a day when you'll connect directly with God through speech. Talking is a basic method of how we as people connect to others and we want to assure ourselves that we're using that power in our daily relationship with God. Create a time when you can be quietly contemplative and meditative while reaching out to speak to God and develop your godliness (using the nighttime silence we talked of before is a great time). It's a uniquely personal relationship so feel free to speak to God as a personal friend, partner and parent. Let Him know your thoughts and feelings, share you successes and failures and what you're working on to grow for that day.

However, DON'T MAKE GOD INTO AN ATM MACHINE. Don't reduce prayer to asking for goodies. So much of prayer seems to center around what we can get from God. I, too ask God for health and well-being. It surely shows my belief that God has power over my well-being. But only using prayer as a wish list meeting will never allow the beautiful relationship that's in store for you. Bring God into your inner circle of thoughts and feelings. Use prayer to develop a real relationship.

It was about seven and three quarters years ago I stopped praying to God for money. My three month old twin had bacterial meningitis and the statisticians had plans for an early grave. It was then I recognized that every moment is precious and my moments with God fell into the same category. If I was to spend time with Him from now on, I would only focus on meaningful discussion, not money. I wouldn't waste a second trying to get money out of

Him anymore (understanding of course, I wasn't in a financial position where I'd be asking for money for basic needs to feed my children or pay for medicines but rather be asking for money to supply me with "extras"). Much more money has come since and I laugh about with God, He must see me as quite immature at times in my deep quest to find more time with Him. But He knows I love Him dearly and only want to be closer and closer to Him.

Talking to God, God's Talking To You

Talking to God is my personal declaration that He and I have a personal relationship. The fact that God will take the time to listen to me whenever I want Him to makes me feel loved. Only a loving parent or a respectful partner would always be willing to listen. I know God is always listening. Sometimes if I make a request He'll say "no" or not even respond right away as any loving parent or partner might. But ultimately, He's there for me and listening. And Talking... Okay, here's where it might get scary for you (I mean how I'm going to sound). But consider so many of your greatest ideas. How did you think of them? Mine just pop into my head. I remember once, it was about three in the morning on a Saturday, my Sabbath, when I'm really immersed in pleasant family and spiritual time. I was pacing thinking about how I could help others in the area of children of divorce. I had already created my Sandcastles Program but it was limited to those areas that ran my programming. And then it dawned on me-take everything I've learned from these fabulous kids and families and write a book so anyone can learn from them. It was one of my most meaningful ideas and perhaps it was an easy thought now looking back. But for me, never having written a book and having no clue where to start finding an agent or publisher, it was a pretty out there idea. Did I think of it? Could it be that I was really connected to my soul, and together with God a message came my way? I like to refer to this as Godspeak.

Every great idea comes from somewhere. You can think about it and think about it all you want but ultimately it comes down to that split second where the idea just pops into your head. God isn't just listening, He's talking to you and helping you all of the time. And God is there to help you bring out the best in you. He has incredible trust. He'll give you a hunch, a gut feeling, a sixth sense. He'll offer you signs, large and small, that'll let you know He's with you and in synch. You just have to be able to feel the signs and learn the language of Godspeak. Oddly, He'll even aid you in developing ideas that might be harmful to you and others. Parents do that sometimes. They help their children develop in areas even though the parent might disagree or feel it's not in their child's best interest. Love will do that to you. God too, wants to be close and is willing to communicate with you even when you're using His ideas to hurt others.

Now I don't mean He wants you to do it or because He is not only your parent but also your creator and architect of the world, He might test you hoping that you can develop into a greater, more spiritual person. Sometimes you might keep the lines of communication open with your child who is doing harmful things to himself or others because you feel that if you cut off ties the child will never have a chance at growing and getting better. God too is willing to hang in there or else the person will never have a chance at changing because genuine change depends on his ability to connect with godliness. So God will hang in there and entertain harmful ideas with the hope that as long as the communication is there, the person might change and show his inner strength and godliness. It's only when we turn our backs completely on people that they have no chance, as seen by the following.

There is a Talmudic discussion about a rebellious son that is discussed in the Torah. A child at a very specific age (about 12 and a half) who steals very specific amounts of wine and meat from his parents and has very specific similarities in his parents AND has both of his parents bring him to the Jewish court, can receive the death penalty because it is declared by God that these ingredients will definitely lead to this young boy murdering one day as an adult. The Talmud explains that the requirements are so rigid that there never was a case where such a penalty was given (One rabbi in the Talmud claims to have seen the grave of one). But the Talmud explains that the Torah wrote about the concept in order to teach us about parenting. One question that a Rabbi explaining the Talmud asks is why it's necessary that both parents drag this child to the court. If he has done everything exactly as it's stated in the Torah then it shouldn't matter who brings him to the court yet alone BOTH parents.

This Rabbi explains a beautiful principle about parenting and the issue we're now discussing about why God hangs in there even with people who are up to no good. He explains that if only one parent brings the boy to court it means that the other parent doesn't want to. And if one parent still has

Prayer

hope for the child then you can't kill him because that hope is what could avoid his becoming a murderer later on. As long as one parent has hope and wants to keep trying, it's possible that the boy will turn himself around, find his soul and change. God talks to all of us and is hoping that we will not let Him and ourselves down. This concept of Godspeak-even if it's a harmful idea-shows God's faith in us and His desire to give us free choice. As discussed before, God needs to allow people to manage their relationship with God in their own way or else we could never be His partner.

How else might God be talking to you? Don't things sometimes happen that just seem like a sign? Don't things just go so smoothly at times that you just wonder if God is smiling on you? Well, He is. He's sending you all kinds of messages that you have to be spiritual enough to hear. Have you ever listened to nature? Have you ever just sat and heard the wind-the rusting of leaves-the harmony of birds or crickets speak to you? I've sat at the beach and focused on the sound of the wind and how it changes with every movement of my head. I know there's a scientific reason, how it's striking your eardrum… But you can hear so much in that wind. You can hear a world of godliness in the crashing waves, the thunder and raindrops. Can you hear it? It's just a matter of recognizing God's voice. Sometimes we don't hear things even with people.

One of my dearest friends is Fred Rogers of *Mister Rogers' Neighborhood*. I say *is* because even after his passing, his friendship lives in me. I didn't know he was so ill and one week before his passing he responded to an email of mine (we kept up regularly through email and of course if you knew Fred, you wouldn't be surprised that one week before his passing even when he had so much going on, he'd take the time to respond to my email) with, "I am eternally grateful for your friendship." Now I thought nothing of it because Fred was given to loving, poetic phrases. But after his passing I retrieved that email and "heard" his message for the first time. Hearing is in the ears of the beholder. We have selective hearing. You can start to hear Godspeak in many ways as soon as you focus on God's voice.

Living Many Lives At Once-Don't Let Time and Space Stand In Your Way

As I write this many things become clearer to me. I've always known that connection takes us far beyond the simple matters in life but everyday I'm realizing how much more so. It seems that through connection, our lives develop. With these ever developing connections, obstacles move out of our way and a powerful spirituality begins to lead us. Time and space no longer apply in the same way when we are connected. For example, it's obvious that we have loved ones who we've only known a short while but can't imagine life without-we feel that we've loved these people so much longer than the real time measured by our clock. There are moments when I am mystified that a short 10 years ago, I didn't have my youngest twin boys in my life or that 19 years ago, I hadn't met my wife and of course the list goes on for each of my children and every person I love. Love is a miracle because we can use it to connect deep within our souls where time and space cannot limit us. You love your spouse, parent and child regardless of whether they live down the block or across the world-even if they no longer live here on earth.

Time and space are simply creations that God gave us in order to offer the consistency and structure that we need to properly navigate life. But make no mistake; they are creations, not absolutes. They are here to enhance our lives with their predictability, not to limit us. That's why everyone should do a little time/space jumping now and then. Don't give in to the limitations of time and space. Today you only have 24 hours but you can do something in a millisecond that will positively affect millions of hours. Think large, think timeless, think forever. Consider your Inner Name-not just here today, but tomorrow, after your death, forever... Don't act for today alone. Consider forever... what are you doing for your forever soul? How could you take little seconds and create from them meaningful moments that transcend time? How could you give more meaning to a second than someone who spends their years of hours plugging away leading a life of quiet desperation?

Hold your child in a way that lets her know your holding her forever. Focus, soulbreathe, can you feel it deep in yourself? Hug your spouse in a way that tells him no matter when or where, this hug is always going on-a hug that's alive in its own reality-as one consistent moment. *This is how we enrich life, by living many moments at the same time. Why live one life when you can be living many?* You can be away from your spouse right now; learning, growing, producing and still feel the hug you received last week. Now you have many moments ganging up to offer you a richer moment. Imagine that when a loved one passes, she is still with you, loving you, advising you, watching over you like always. That moment is everlasting and just added to the mix of new moments you have. So your birth certificate might say you're a certain age but you've compounded so many moments that you have potential to live an infinite amount of more seconds than your age tells. You've heard of compounded interest. *This is* compounded living, *when you're developing upon each earlier moment causing the new moments to bear greater returns.*

The Torah let's us know in many places that time and space is never intended to limit us but there is one interaction that clearly tells us about this secret of time. God commands Moses to tell Pharaoh that if he continues to refuse to free the Jewish slaves, the final plague of the first born will strike at midnight. Moses follows this command but changes one thing. Moses says the plague will strike "around midnight." Clearly, Moses must have some compelling reason to change God's instruction. Jewish tradition explains that Moses (being God's PR man as outlined before) decided unilaterally to make the change so that if the Egyptians get the exact time of midnight wrong they won't stand there even if but for a second thinking God made some mistake or isn't able to follow through. Whatever the exact reason for this change the simple question is why would the Egyptians not know when midnight was exactly? They had timing mechanisms that kept excellent track of time. God is teaching us a lesson about time.

What is midnight? Consider it. Is there such a thing? When the clock strikes midnight, it merely has counted over to the next seconds beginning after 12 a.m. In other words there is no such thing as MID night. There's no actual time in between the millisecond before 12 and after 12. Either you're borrowing from the millisecond before 12 or the millisecond after 12. We call it midnight but it's nothing more than 1, 2, or 9 o'clock, it's 12 o'clock. It's not even the middle of the night unless you live somewhere where the sun sets consistently at 6 p.m. and rises at 6 a.m. But God created a midnight, a time that rose above the normal calculations of our world. That's why Moses says around midnight because the Egyptians would know there is no point called midnight and therefore would look askance at Moses' apparent ignorant understanding of time.

But what Moses knew was that there are periods of time that stand still and these moments are alive and breathing in a way that makes them move outside the standard of normal time. Midnight is one of them that is consistently available and given to godliness which is why spiritual, other worldly occurrences happen at midnight: the Jews are freed beginning their holy journey toward their deeper inner name, years later King David is awoken at midnight when his harp plays as the wind dances through his window and he writes his deeply spiritual book of Psalms, and who can forget that at midnight, Cinderella is returned to her old self, forced to find her self-value and love in her real self unaided by fancy spells.

Living Instead of Commemorating

The Jewish calendar speaks volumes to this concept of not having a shallow vision of time. On Passover night when Jews celebrate the exodus from Egypt, we do many things to help us feel as though we are slaves and then exiting to our new lives. But it's not a game of symbolism. The Talmud instructs that it is incumbent on all Jews that they see themselves as if they were slaves and then freed. Toward that end, bitter herbs are eaten causing many to have tears in their eyes and some have a custom of putting matzos on their backs and walking around the table signifying the flight from Egypt. Every Jewish holiday carries the same concept of not merely commemorating but reliving these moments. It is because these moments are somehow always recurring. Our souls don't know about time in the same way our hearts and brains do. Our souls can plug into moments from the past and in the future and live them because souls can connect in that way. Maybe it was a hug felt three thousand years ago by my great great….. grandmother who eventually gave that hug to me in some way that I can tap into from feeling the same earth or reading the same story or singing the same traditional songs. But I can feel it. I can sense it and that moment can be as real to me, even more real than seeing with my own eyes today.

Somehow that only our souls can feel and our minds cannot fathom, everything is happening at once. When you can feel a hug today in your heart that was given to you forty years ago, you're not merely remembering. You could be feeling it because it is still happening today. The same feelings of love are alive miraculously and the godliness in that love still breathes. To God everything is somehow happening all at once. It's one large picture so that in our souls we can feel all of history today. Consider dejavu. Is it real? Perhaps you were in that place before, perhaps your soul connects to it because it's felt connected to that situation. Could it be your soul feels connected because it lived before in another body? Or part of your soul was part of another soul at that time? Or maybe what was happening before in that place is still happening and you're connecting to it for some reason. Anything is possible with godliness.

We think finite-every second is turning into history. But in truth, all life and all moments are immortal and building their own being. A kindness is forever, not only because it affects the recipient who might change his life some way after receiving the kindness; but because that kindness has tapped into a soul which is immortal and doesn't know about history. Time doesn't pass to God, it just is… All the soul can feel is change, growth, development. It can sense movement but is not bound by time. It doesn't lose its moments. Moments attach to your soul and you become a new vibrant being. This means we can tap into any time, any person of our past and any moment. It's takes quite a spiritual giant to be able to feel this regularly and again, there isn't one thing you can do to force yourself to see the "fire." But the process of enhancing and nurturing your Inner Name will lead you to see what will become obvious. *Time is not clicking away. Time is building.* Whenever you are adding spirituality to life, you are creating the world with something special and new because the world is creating itself every moment. Creation hasn't passed us by. The Talmud says that anyone who keeps the Jewish Sabbath is as if he creates the world with God. He is actually creating the world because the world is still being created from its inception and you and I can place ingredients into it that no one else has, ingredients that will make us architects of the world and forever change its composition.

We have all the power we need and want to learn to focus our spiritual energy to develop our own unique way of using and experiencing it. Each of us can do what we need in order to see far beyond the clock on the wall. There'll come the time when you can feel it, know it and not be able to necessarily show it to everyone else. We can tap into the past and future with our focus on godliness. We can feel people who have passed, people who will come across our paths in the future. We can love in a way that is far beyond the heartfelt meaning that we may have mistakenly thought was the best we could do. You are a powerful source of godliness and you can take that and make it dance forever and build in the hands of others who'll connect with you. When you can't believe you love your child this much and it's only been a short time you've known her, guess again. In your soul, you're a part of everyone else and have known each other forever.

That's the point. We are all connected through our godliness. When someone did something godly three thousand years ago, it had some direct impact on each of us because our souls are a part of God. If your soul has been around forever, it was around when every other soul made a spiritual move and thus affected you. You can tap into its affect and feel that moment happening in some way but uniquely in the way that it personally affected your soul. That means you can feel the past and future but only as it relates to your unique Name because every soul is affected by life in a different way. I imagine that when your parent does something spiritual it affects your soul more than if my parent did a similar thing. So we tend to be able to connect to spiritual moments of our past, present or future that relate more to our unique selves, whether that's means we can feel more of other's spirituality because we are closer connected in family, heritage, type of personality, or even simply physical place in the world. Obviously, everyone has his or her unique ability to connect. But help yourself by imagining certain scenes.

Picture what it might have felt like to be the person who built your home. Visit historical sights with the childlike innocence of sensing what it might have been like for someone like you to have been there at that time, or the feelings of a famous person you know of. As I edit this my children are in front of me writing about what it might have felt like to be Patrick Henry (We recently returned from a vacation in Colonial Williamsburg). Read letters you might have of your grandparents and study their pictures. You may never have known them but you do know them in your soul, your Inner Name is drawn on them in part. If you are drawn to a certain period in history, study it, visit it, open yourself to it. There's probably a soulful reason you feel drawn to that period. Likewise, if you feel drawn to a building, spend some time in it. If you have a flower that seems to call out to you, plant it and smell it regularly. If you love a certain activity with your child or spouse, engage in it with love. Do the things that sing to you in a way and all along, soulbreathe and you'll begin to connect to different periods of time that escape the boundaries of what we refer to as time.

This places an important goal in front of us. Imagine the potential you have. With every spiritual move you can be building moments that will always be alive. At the same time, we are able to wreak havoc with our souls zapping our spiritual energy forever. It's a serious but loving task. In any love relationship we can do so much to change the relationship forever in a positive way and of course in a negative way as well.

True Love is Being Able to Say I'm Sorry and I Forgive You

But luckily, God is more understanding than any of us. Even after ignoring Him, He still offers us an open invitation to develop a new relationship with Him. We can contend with our mistakes-we are able to approach God and say, "I'm sorry."

As further proof of our real down to earth relationship we have with God, He discusses repentance with us. *Repentance is feeling genuinely sorry that I've done something to cause some distance between me and God.* It's no different than saying sorry to anyone. I have to understand what I did that hurt the other person, apologize, and have a legitimate plan of how I'll change my life so that I don't continue to hurt the other person in a similar fashion. Asking forgiveness is part of every healthy ongoing relationship. It's as if you're saying, "I'm trying to relate to you and see that I've hurt you and made myself difficult to love."

It's equally important to be forgiving. I'll never forget the moving apology written by Elie Wiesel to God in the New York Times Op Ed page a few years ago on Rosh Hashanah. A survivor of the Holocaust, Mr. Wiesel has written about his angst with God. After years of anger and even questioning his own belief in God, his ability to offer forgiveness was indeed godly of him. I recall sharing with friends of mine how moved I was. I was crying because of the spirituality I felt at the moment. But one friend was belittling of the forgiveness granted. "Who does he think he is that he can offer forgiveness to God." I understood this point. I don't believe it was about calling God a "wrongdoer." It was saying to God something like, "Look, You allowed something to happen that I'll never understand. And that caused great distance between us. I was angry. I felt You hurt me deeply. But now I can see it in a different way as well as having seen what you've done in other ways since then that has helped me bridge the gap." It was an honest portrayal of a genuine relationship with God, through thick and thin. Some terribly unfortunate things happen in life that will challenge our relationship with God. Those moments are the times when we can still work to find peace in the "fire" we've seen even if we can't see the "fire" at that moment because of our grief or pain. Seeing the deeper spiritual side of life in the past reminds us that there is some greater plan that we can't personally see, yet. We remember that parents do things that children can't imagine are for their benefit even though that's the parent's sole motivation.

It is moving how many people find their Inner Name through tragedy. Unfortunately, the world keeps us so busy that too often we stay somewhat blind to the "fire" that we carry within. Then when life spins out of control and doesn't make sense, we search for something deeper than shallow gains to explain and navigate life. We begin with our godliness because it's there in a very natural way. The search for your Inner Name isn't complicated, only opening yourself up to it is. Once we let go of the worldly diversions, God is staring at us from within our own selves. And He's never angry about not being close to us before. He understands-no different than a parent who would gladly welcome back her flesh and blood after years of being ignored even if that parent thought the child was at fault.

But why wait to find our inner godliness until we're forced to through some hardship that causes us to be suddenly lost in the world? Being in touch with our godliness will lessen any hardship or challenge because as life throws us curveballs we'll be defining life in a far richer, soulful way. We will literally feel less pain in times of struggle automatically because we'll see the "fire" and never feel lost.

Death is Just Another Beginning

When a loved one passes away, it's always a time of struggle. Yet it can serve as a time of ultimate understanding of how souls know no boundaries of time and space. We can "feel" people who've passed away. I don't only mean recall what advice they would give us in a given situation or how they would've acted. I mean feel it, feel a certain warmth that's nurturing us when we need it. We've all heard so many stories of how something wonderful happened to an individual and that person just "knew" that it was added guidance and help from a loved one who had passed away.

There's a story about this young lady who had a wonderful relationship with her gentle father. He was older when she was born so he soon retired and spent much of his time with her. One of his favorite hobbies was butterfly watching. For years they planted butterfly gardens and stood still for endless moments waiting and watching stunning butterflies make their way across their path. One year after he passed she deeply missed her Dad, found herself financially strapped and was experiencing a messy divorce. The day came when she lost health insurance for her son and herself and couldn't find affordable coverage. She worked for a jeweler and basically depended on commissions. Finally building up the courage to ask her boss for a loan, he refused but told her as an incentive, he'd double her commission on the next piece of jewelry she'd sell that day. My friend excused herself to the back of the store and had a conversation with her Dad pleading to him for help.

It was less than thirty minutes when a customer entered to purchase an expensive pendant for his wife. It was the largest sale she had ever made. What kind of pendant? Yes, it had diamonds and rubies but that wasn't what convinced her that her Dad had everything to do with sending this customer to her at this moment. It was the *type* of pendant the gentleman had requested. The customer who entered the store told of his wife's fascination with what she considered the most beautiful creature known to the world. That's right, he wanted a diamond pendant in the shape of a butterfly. It was three months later on her father's birthday that her son was hurt in a car accident and was saved potentially due to the private health insurance allowing for the best immediate medical attention.

Everyone has their own stories if they're aware enough to be looking for the signs, the "fire." Sometimes, a loved one makes it so easy for you to see and sometimes it's more subtle. But the bottom line is that souls never die. Death is the end of the

Death Is Just Another Beginning

stage when your soul is encased in your body. That's it. There are people who've spoken to the dead in some fashion because the souls are as vibrant if not more so than ever. You might not believe that anyone has communicated with someone who's passed away. Perhaps you explain it as a form of wish fulfillment dreaming. That's possible of course. But there are stories you just can't explain away. I have a personal friend who was away on vacation when her Dad passed away. Now he wasn't particularly sick so she wasn't expecting him to die that night. She was away so she didn't get called until hours after he passed. But she had a dream where her Dad was standing with his elbows on his coffin (at the time of the dream she couldn't figure out what the table was, she thought it was a poker table because her Dad liked to play cards but after hearing the news of his passing she thought back and realized it was his coffin), and said to her, "Honey, I'm checking out." She woke up and received the call of her father's passing. That's just one story from a personal friend who I know is not putting me on or getting her facts messed up. There are far more dramatic stories of incredible episodes, including those who've died on the surgery table and returned to life.

Whenever I'm around spiritual people who are close to passing away, there's never fear or anything but peace. They just know it'll be as miraculous as every other part of life. When Abraham lets it be known to his son Isaac, who is 36 years old at the time, that Abraham plans to slaughter him, there is great peace with Isaac. So much so that there is very little mention of Isaac during the entire story. It seems to be Abraham's challenge. Rather, Abraham navigated life through kindness so killing his own child was a struggle, a struggle he overcame out of love for his Inner Name and spirituality. But for Isaac, there seems to be no challenge at all. He navigates life through his spiritual strength and although he might have preferred to continue living in his present state and grow spiritually down here, he knew there was more spiritual growth to look forward to in any event. Whenever God said time was up, he was completely at peace with it.

Frankly, I've had my share of death anxiety. I've suffered at times, lost some sleep over the fear of death, the unknown-not being as I'm used to being. I've talked to scholarly rabbis and brilliant people about it and they've all helped me have some clearer understanding. In fact when I was 18, I waited for seven months to have an audience with a rabbi who I had great respect for in order to discuss the afterlife. He helped me immensely with his understanding of what happens to us after death. But all of the explanations don't do it. Trying to resolve spiritual issues with my head never works.

For me there's only one thing that relieves this anxiety. When I get in touch with my spirituality, pray and talk to God, study the Torah and its inspiring stories of my ancestors, involve myself with spiritual pursuits, focus on spiritual moments; those days are full with everything but death anxiety. I don't even have to work at keeping my anxiety at bay. It's simply as if it never existed. When I see the "fire," life is clear and I'm choosing to be more alive than ever. In that sense of being extremely alive, my soul is nourished, I'm at one with my Inner Name, and there is never any sense of dying. I am simply too alive to ever die-my immortal connection to godliness is burning in a peaceful way that tells me, I will be alive forever within Him.

When a love one passes away, you can know that they are not just a memory but a living, breathing being that is in you. Every moment you shared, every loving gesture connected your souls even more and that connection is immortal. You live within that moment forever as you add onto it many more moments. Time stands still within your spirit as it is reliving every hug, every kiss, every touch, every shared moment. Time is on your side.

Epilogue

Well, it's hard to end because there really isn't an end. But I feel I've learned along with you and that's what I wanted most out of this. I never wanted to teach you anything but simply think out loud with you, connecting in our own way. Take me with you as I'm sure I will take you and your spirituality along with me. I don't know who you are but it doesn't matter whether you're my child, grandchild, close friend or stranger. Now we are immortal spiritual friends and, as my dear friend Fred Rogers wrote to me days before his passing, "for that I am eternally grateful."

There's a moving story in the Talmud about two rabbis who disagreed on the interpretation of a certain law. Suddenly a heavenly voice called out stating that one of the rabbis was correct in his opinion. But the other rabbis present agreed that the heavenly voice had no decision making (or swaying of opinion) capabilities. These rabbis quoted a statement in the Torah where God said, "It (Torah) is not in heaven." God states that people should not be saying that spirituality is hard to attain. God tells us it's not stuck on some mountain top, far out at sea or in the heavens where one can't reach it. The rabbis extended this thinking to explain that even if a heavenly voice screams out an answer to a legal question, it is ignored.

God wants humans to develop the world *with* Him. God's looking for partners, not infants. He's put Himself into every one of us. Don't look in the heavens. Look for the "fire" inside of you-it's right there where God left it. Be godly, Be a partner, Be the miracle.

I just returned from a sunset. I'm vacationing with my family on the west coast of Florida where I've done so every summer for eighteen years. Today my Mother-in-law called me, my wife spoke to my Mom and Dad, my sister-in-law left a kind message for me. Moments ago I walked along a beach with my soulmate, our five children and three dogs. On one side of the horizon the sun melted into the gulf while on the other horizon, two rainbows dwarfed me. My daughter asked me why God used the rainbow as a symbol of potential doom. She referred to a Jewish teaching that understands the rainbow as a statement from God outlining His dismay with people. It's as if God is saying He'd be justified in destroying humankind but he promised Noah he'd never do that again and offered Noah the rainbow as a symbol of this promise. According to this explanation, my daughter wanted to know why a scarier symbol wasn't used by God to motivate us to change and grow more spiritually.

I tell her I think it's because God wants to motivate His loved ones through the beautiful miracles He has given us. He wants us to love Him, not fear Him, be that partner of His, not His terrified slaves. He shows that rainbow to tell us, "Look what is here and what is in store for you at every moment that you grow your godliness." The most stunning piece of nature that can be seen from anywhere, the rainbow is a symbol of what can be absolutely right with our spiritual world. As my daughter and I discuss this, my three younger boys are delightfully kicking up water as their whole bodies and spirits are consumed with the moment of family love and togetherness in a special place we continue to return to. My seventeen year old son who loves the movies says to no one in particular, "Who needs to be at the movies when God creates this kind of picture," and points out to me a certain cloud structure at yet a different point of the horizon that is miraculous to him. My wife and I walk hand in hand in a dance that has become as easy and natural as walking by myself.

And I am intoxicated with this life of mine as I walk so close to my loved ones- the ones I see with my eyes, the ones I feel in my heart-as I step closer to my Inner Name-melting into a single moment that I will live in forever and take with me wherever I may go-much the way the sun has just melted into the water and will continue to do so forever. I'm not waiting for Heaven, I'll take as many pieces of it that I can right now. The night is here and tonight I am clearer than ever. Thank you.

About the Author

Rabbi M. Gary Neuman is a Florida-state licensed mental health counselor, creator of the internationally recognized Sandcastles Program for children of divorce, and author of *Helping Your Kids Cope with Divorce the Sandcastles Way (Random House)* and *Emotional Infidelity, How to Affair-Proof Your Marriage and Other Secrets to a Great Marriage (Three Rivers Press)*.

His work has received national media coverage including multiple appearances on *The Oprah Show, Today, The View*, and National Public Radio's *Talk of the Nation* as well as appearances on *Dateline*, NBC *Nightly* News, CBS *Weekend* News, and *Good Morning America*. He has been written about in numerous publications including *People, Time, Parents, Washington Post, Chicago Tribune, Baltimore Sun*, and *Miami Herald*. He has won various awards including the Gold Excellence

Award from Parents Publications of America for his internationally syndicated column, "Changing Families," and the Significant Contributions to Families & Children award from the Florida Association for Marriage & Family Therapy. He is a member of the advisory board of Parents Magazine.

Rabbi Neuman tours the country, speaking about marital and family issues, spirituality and his 2x2 corporate seminars. He maintains a private practice in Miami, Florida, where he sees adults, children, and families. He lives with his wife and five children in Miami Beach, Florida.

If you would like information about any of his seminars, or would like to share your own spiritually inspiring stories or ideas, please write to:
Rabbi M. Gary Neuman, LMHC
Post Office Box 402691
Miami Beach, Florida 33140-0691
or visit www.mgaryneuman.com